A New Beginning

by Ed Clark
Libertarian Candidate
for President of the
United States

Library of Congress Catalog Card Number 80-68831
International Standard Book Number 0-89803-047-1

With the deepest appreciation, this book is dedicated to the great fighters for libertarian causes of past and present, especially John Locke, Thomas Jefferson, Tom Paine, Frederick Douglass, Richard Cobden and John Bright, Rose Wilder Lane, Ludwig von Mises, F. A. Hayek, and Murray Rothbard, and to the men and women who are carrying the fight for liberty into the future.

Introduction

The Introductory chapter of this book by Ed Clark, the Libertarian candidate for the presidency in this year of 1980, would be, as the saying goes, worth the price of the book. It lays out, objectively, in historical context, and in lean, clean English, the basic political, economic, and cultural problems of America which affect politics and which are affected by politics. It then defines the Libertarian approach to government and politics—particularly as distinguished from that of the Republicans and the Democrats, the two legally established (and publicly financed) political parties of the United States.

But Ed Clark goes beyond the presentation of Libertarian philosophy and criticism of the established parties. In the ensuing chapters, he applies his principles to major national issues and then proposes courses of action which are more specific and directed than most of the "planks" likely to appear in the Republican or Democratic platforms.

The American electorate would be well served if other presidential candidates, including independents, could be moved to write and publish books, as Ed Clark has done, which actually set forth a political philosophy and proposals for dealing with major problems. Perhaps, then, the election of a President would be decided on a better basis than newspaper headlines, TV commercials, staged debates, purposeless government-financed conventions, news photos of candidates walking into fish ponds or shaking hands with airport crowds, public medical reports and income tax returns, and interviews in which candidates discuss politics, religion, lust, and love.

The emergence of the Libertarian Party as an increasingly viable political alternative to the two state-approved parties is to be applauded, regardless of whether or not one agrees with every aspect of their program. The fact is that the Federal

Election Campaign Act has greatly restricted open politics in America. That the fresh breeze of dissent from the status quo still survives in the form of this feisty and determined party and its articulate candidate for president is a tribute to the American spirit.

I am pleased to commend Ed Clark's intelligent and challenging book to the attention of all who seek a new beginning.

Eugene McCarthy
Washington, D. C.
August, 1980

A Note to the Reader

This small book addresses some very large problems. If I'd tried to do justice to all of the issues of this election, I'd have had to write an entire library of books—which would have significantly interfered with the day-in, day-out campaigning I've been doing to bring Libertarian ideas to the people of this country.

In this book I've tried to give an overview of the Libertarian approach to our particularly pressing problems. It may be that Libertarians don't have 100% of the answers to all of our problems, but I'm certain that we have the basic answer. That answer is explained in the book, but I can give you a hint: it's a startling, radical answer which was discovered centuries ago by such people as Thomas Jefferson and Tom Paine. It's old wisdom, confirmed and revalidated by the best of today's research and evidence.

Naturally, I hope that, after you've read what I have to say, you'll find that you fundamentally agree with me. You may even conclude, as many Libertarians have, that you've been a Libertarian all your life and didn't know it, and that you've finally found an expression of your own basic convictions. But agree or not, I'm fully confident that you'll find Libertarian ideas provocative and challenging, and I'd be delighted to hear from you about them. Write to me at Clark for President Headquarters, 2300 Wisconsin Avenue NW, Washington, D.C. 20007.

The Libertarian movement is by now much larger than the Clark for President campaign—there are over 500 Libertarian candidates this year, running for local, state, and federal office. And our ideas come from many, many people as well. As I present this book to the American public, I'd like to thank my friends who helped me in writing it, including David Boaz, Ralph Raico, Joan Kennedy Taylor, Chris Hocker, Sheldon Richman, Roy Childs, Tom Palmer, and Ed Crane. Of course, in keeping with the Libertarian principle of taking responsibility for one's own actions, such mistakes as might be in the book are mine and not theirs.

I would ask the reader particularly to indulge my forecast of Ronald Reagan and Jimmy Carter as the nominees of their parties this year. Political forecasting is always a dangerous art, and never more so than now, when the level of disenchantment with the established parties has reached the level of an epidemic. In writing this book prior to the Republican and Democratic conventions, I have chosen to criticize the likely nominees by name; but I want to make clear my opinion that there is no other potential nominee in either party who would change my fundamental view of the problems we face and the need to solve them through a totally different approach. It shouldn't be difficult for the reader, once having caught the thread of my ideas and proposals, to see that my indictments of Reagan and Carter would apply to any other Republican or Democratic nominee, differing somewhat in details but not at the core of my criticisms.

We are a relatively new organization. But we are motivated by an idea, and, as Victor Hugo said, there is nothing so powerful as an idea whose time has come. You'll be hearing more and more about us Libertarians both in this campaign and in the years ahead. Here's your chance to get in on the ground floor.

Ed Clark
Los Angeles, California
August, 1980

Contents

CHAPTER 1:

What Ever Happened to the American Dream?

It has been said that an American today who is uninterested in politics is like a drowning man who is indifferent to water. Everywhere we look we see the effects of our politicians at work: taxes completely out of control; inflation destroying our living standards; the threat of war; the energy crisis; civil liberties and personal freedoms endangered; schools that don't teach; poverty that continues despite endless "poverty programs"; and all the rest. There is no American untouched by the damage politicians have done and continue to do.

A concerned person who conscientiously keeps up with the news must sometimes despair. Where are the solutions to come from? Does it make sense to trust the same kind of men who brought us where we are now? Every election, our political leaders hire the best consultants that money can buy (that *your* money can buy, since the major party campaigns are now "publicly" financed), to give themselves a political face-lift, and somehow convince us that they're offering something new. Every minor difference of opinion among them, every nuance of style or personality, is blown all out of proportion, as if they were differences that mattered. The politicians offer, in other words, what I have called "the politics of manipulation."

And yet our problems continue and multiply, to the point where Americans—who would have believed it?—are beginning to lose faith in "the happy ending." Why? Why can't our leaders find real solutions? Is there some fundamental flaw in the system within which they operate? And, most importantly, is there a way to correct this flaw, to change the system so that we can have reason to hope again?

I contend that the fundamental flaw in the system is the notion that the entity that we call "government" is inherently more capable of solving our problems than are individuals or voluntary associations of individuals.

Consider the following examples:

● In Rochester, New York, in 1976, the husband-and-wife team of Paul and Patricia Brennan started up a mail delivery service. Originally motivated by frustration with the inefficiency of the U.S. Postal Service, the Brennans found that they could deliver mail within the city more quickly and at lower cost than could the government—and still make a profit. They soon discovered, however, that competing with first class government mail delivery was a *crime*; they were prosecuted, their business was shut down, and they lost their final legal appeal in federal court.

● For 25 years, an informal chain of privately financed community programs known as "Meals on Wheels" delivered prepared food to the homes of poor, disabled, and elderly people in many American cities. In 1979, the federal government decided to initiate its own "Meals on Wheels" program, at first intending to expand and "improve upon" the existing service. The result, however, was to drive voluntary programs out of business while failing to adequately provide meals for those who needed them—and who were getting them before government entered the picture.

● Today, Marva Collins, a former public school teacher, operates a private school in the middle of a Chicago black ghetto. Her Westside Preparatory School takes children whom the public schools labeled "learning disabled," "disturbed," or even "retarded," and teaches them to read, write, and discuss ideas at levels far above normal for their age and grade. "My students learn that tax dollars will not solve their problems, that we together must do that," says Ms. Collins. Her school survives on modest monthly tuitions supplemented by private contributions. To preserve the school's independence, she has rejected a financial grant offered by the federal government.

In all of the above examples, the lines were clearly drawn between individual freedom and the power of government. In each case, the individuals involved rejected government as a problem-solver and instead chose voluntary, honest, and peaceful means to get things done.

In each instance, the approach taken by the individuals involved can be described as a *libertarian* approach. In the present political context, people who consistently prefer to choose such an approach are *Libertarians*. And the political organization which advocates this voluntaristic approach to America's problems is the *Libertarian Party*.

Libertarians are, of course, concerned with the rights of individuals to deliver mail in competition with the U.S. Postal Service, or to organize private meal delivery programs, or to establish private schools free from government supervision. But more than this, Libertarians view such situations as examples of a method which will work for America regardless of the issue at hand—as well as examples of government's blind and arrogant opposition to this method. My campaign for President brings the Libertarian approach to critical economic, social, and foreign policy issues—and shows how the Libertarian alternative can hope to solve America's problems.

The Libertarian approach—the Libertarian alternative—is a unique political philosophy which has never before been fully implemented in American history, although it traces its roots to the classical liberal tradition of Thomas Jefferson, George Mason, and Thomas Paine. The Libertarian Party is a unique political phenomenon which has shown an impressive rate of steady growth since its inception in 1972. Political commentator Nick Thimmesch has called it "far more creative, diverse in approach, and intellectually stimulating than either the Democrats or Republicans."

People are turning to the Libertarian approach—the party, its candidates, and its ideas—in greater and greater numbers for two reasons: First, Libertarians offer a real hope of solving problems. Second, the present political lineup of Republicans and Democrats has utterly failed.

From the time they enter first grade, and even before, Americans are taught that there are two political parties in America—Republicans and Democrats—and that there are two political philosophies—liberal and conservative. Yet most Americans are hard pressed to describe the differences between

3

Republicans and Democrats, and even have difficulty defining what is "conservative" and what is "liberal." Generally speaking, Democrats are perceived as being more "liberal" than Republicans (but not always, and not in some parts of the country); they tend to favor more government intervention in the economy than Republicans do; they tend to favor government spending on "have-nots" rather than the "haves"; and they appear to be somewhat more tolerant of divergent lifestyles and new social movements. Republicans, on the other hand, are regarded as more "conservative"; more likely to extend "help" to business; less willing to spend money on government social programs; and more intent on upholding "traditional American values" than on permitting social change.

But even these generalities, broad as they are, fail to describe most individual politicians of the Republican or Democratic parties. Rather, most such candidates and elected officials jump from position to position, from issue to issue, in search of a safe middle ground, without discernible ideology, philosophy, or principle—and then cynically try to label their scramblings "pragmatic" or even "courageous "

This is particularly true of foreign policy, where it's now impossible to tell the players without a scorecard Republicans who at least pay lip-service to "fiscal conservatism" have become patsies for the Pentagon's budgetary demands, while normally free-spending Democrats favor a degree of restraint—but even these roles become jumbled and blurred according to the foreign crisis of the moment. No wonder that, of all our major problems, foreign policy often appears to be the most hopeless.

Many Americans are discovering the fact that the differences between Republicans and Democrats, liberals and conservatives, aren't nearly so striking or important as are their *similarities*. In response to this fact, more and more voters refuse to identify themselves with either of the established parties—33 percent of the electorate in 1980, compared with 20 percent in 1960. And more and more of those eligible to vote are refusing to vote at all, with voter turnout dropping from 63 percent in 1960 to just 54 percent in 1976.

4

As in most things, the American people are wiser and more sophisticated than their leaders when it comes to evaluating traditional two-party politics. While politicians drone on about the "Grand Old Party," or the "party of Jefferson, Jackson, and Franklin Roosevelt" (what a combination!), the voters, even those who still consider themselves nominally Republican or Democratic, are rejecting those parties in massive numbers.

The two established parties are declining because, behind the faded red, white, and blue banners, the brass bands, and the papier-maché donkeys and elephants, lie the tattered remains of ideas and approaches which have failed, regardless of which party or which politician tried to implement them.

For how do traditional politicians view the use of political power? Some sincerely believe in government-as-problem-solver, pinning their faith on the supposition that "if we could only get the right people into government, everything would work out fine." Others, perhaps a majority, are not so naive. They understand only too well that government-imposed solutions are destined to fail, but they continue to play a cynical game of political manipulation, using their power to reward favored individuals and groups at the expense of others. They care little for the rights of individuals, but view people merely as "interest groups" or "voting blocs," the clever manipulation of which will successfully get them through the next election and move them up the ladder of power. The leaders of such interest groups as businessmen, labor unions, or ethnic minorities are often quite willing to go along with this game of manipulation, since it enhances their power and influence in the short run—until some other interest group or voting bloc comes along and shoulders them out of the way. Given this situation—in which the political process is used merely to accumulate power—can we reasonably expect that national problems will be solved by government?

A glance at recent political history shows that America's problems have continued regardless of the party in the White House, at the levers of power. Inflation has risen steadily since 1960, through twelve years of Democratic presidents and eight years of Republicans. Inflation, when it affects those least able to afford it, is in principle no different at the five per cent level

5

than at the 18 per cent level—it merely devastates the incomes of more people, at a faster clip, when at the higher level. Yet no Democrat and no Republican has had the will to stop it.

Over the same period of time, the size of the federal budget—the amount of money raised and spent by the federal government—has doubled roughly every eight years, increasing from $97 billion in 1960 to $620 billion in 1980. Republicans tended to propose somewhat higher budget increases than did Democratic administrations, but, regardless of who was in office, the damage done to our economy and to our take-home pay has continued its steady increase from year to year.

The last twenty years saw the bloody, senseless, and tragic war in Vietnam escalated by Democratic presidents with the enthusiastic approval of both parties in Congress—and saw a Republican president take six years to de-escalate that war to its conclusion, long after it had become a daily blight on the lives of millions of Americans and on the honor of the United States itself. Never in recent times have our basic rights and freedoms been so severely threatened as during that period of "de-escalation," when domestic spying and crackdowns on peaceful dissent became a common occurrence.

Today, the problems of inflation, taxation, war, and threats to basic liberties remain with us—and few would seriously suggest that they will disappear if either the Republicans or the Democrats are in power after the 1980 election.

Worse even than a lack of solutions is the absence even of *hope* for improvement. Lack of hope, acceptance of failure, a feeling that the best we can expect is that things won't get any worse—such a mood threatens to crush the dynamic, free, creative American spirit.

We must constantly remind ourselves what is at stake when we enter the political arena. The political process determines which party and which candidates will fill political offices, and it therefore determines if and how our problems will be solved. It determines whether inflation will continue, at a higher or lower rate—or it can determine that inflation will be stopped. It determines whether government taxing and spending will increase at a faster or slower pace—or it can determine

6

that taxing and spending will be cut and cut again. It determines whether our basic freedoms will be infringed upon to a greater or lesser degree—or it can determine that these freedoms will be recognized as absolute individual rights, not to be violated. It determines whether we will face actual war or only the threat of war—or it can determine that we will establish a new foreign policy of true, lasting peace and security.

Ultimately, the political process determines not just the fate of parties, candidates, and issues, but also the very conditions under which Americans will live. To Libertarians, paramount among these conditions is *freedom*—freedom to live your life as you choose so long as you are not violating the rights of others; freedom to be responsible for the consequences of your own actions; freedom to solve problems, great and small, in voluntary cooperation with others. It is this freedom, after all, for which the United States was founded.

People came to America, from Europe first and then from every corner of the globe, to make a new beginning for themselves, free of the restraints they found in other countries. America's Founders fought a revolution and created a new nation because they wanted to be free—free of the age-old system of government control, high taxes, war, and centralized rule, free to live their own lives, free to speak and write and worship and acquire property and trade. They established a nation based on the rights of life, liberty, and the pursuit of happiness. While there were glaring inconsistencies—particularly the existence of slavery in a nation based on freedom—for the most part these ideals were upheld, and for many years the new nation flourished. But in recent years we have gotten away from the American tradition of freedom. Our political leaders have raised our taxes, regulated our businesses and our personal lives, involved us in foreign wars, and centralized more and more power in Washington. I think it's time to restore the tradition of freedom in America.

Libertarians, holding freedom as our highest political ideal, are creating a totally new alternative to the Republican and Democratic parties, as well as to anyone else who views government as a problem-solver. Traditional politics have failed, but the Libertarian alternative brings the hope of success.

We can only hope to solve America's problems through the relatively simple process of examining each problem, analyzing its effects, identifying its cause, and striking at the root of the problem. To do this will require a willingness to make a significant departure from the politics of the past, and to move forward in a new direction, applying the principles of the American Revolution to the problems of the 1980's.

It's time to strike at the root of our problems. It's time for a new beginning.

CHAPTER 2:

Cutting Government Down to Size

The federal government has become a crushing burden on the American people. For 1981, President Carter has proposed spending $612 billion of our money Under Carter's budget, taxes will increase by $90 billion from 1980 to 1981, including $60 billion in *new* taxes.

I think this budget is much too high. I think taxes are much too high. Our right to spend our own money as we choose is being taken away from us. We are being robbed by an ever-growing federal government with an insatiable appetite for our money.

Today, the average American worker pays 45 percent of his or her income to government. Feudal serfs paid only about 25 percent of their income to their masters, and Americans historically paid only about 10 percent of their income in taxes. As Howard Jarvis, the courageous co-author of Proposition 13, said recently, "The people of·this country want a tax cut. They don't particularly care what the government thinks about it. They think they're being robbed and they are." I agree with Howard Jarvis. We're being robbed and it's time to stop it.

Almost all objective observers agree that federal spending is far too high and that many federal programs are wasteful, unnecessary, ill-conceived, or positively harmful Why, then, does government spending continue to grow?

This is a basic problem of a government-dominated economy. Each new spending program provides major benefits to a small group of people, and imposes relatively small costs on the majority of us. A farm subsidy, for example, may be worth tens of thousands of dollars each to certain farmers, but cost other Americans only a few cents each. The federal bailout for Chrysler is worth $1.5 billion tó Chrysler's management, and may ultimately cost each taxpayer about $20.

In each case the beneficiaries of the program find it worthwhile to lobby for it. They hire a Washington lobbyist, come to Washington themselves, entertain members of Congress, contribute to their re-election campaigns, and mount elaborate public-relations efforts. The taxpayers, on the other hand, stand to lose only a little on each program, so it's not really worth their time to lobby *against* the proposal. A particular program, for example, may cost you $1.25 in taxes, but it costs you $2.00 to call your Congressman just to find out about it. Obviously, it isn't worth the money to you. So Congress, seeing much support and little opposition, passes yet another spending program to benefit the special interests at the expense of all the rest of us.

But these programs quickly add up; and while any one of them may not seem to cost much, the total is staggering—$612 billion for 1981. And it is rising at a frightening pace. Ten years ago the budget was only $211 billion. Four years ago, when President Carter came into office, the budget was $403 billion. It has increased 52 percent—$209 billion—just during Carter's term in office. And an official study by the Congressional Research Service predicts that taxes will continue to soar through the end of the century The study reported that the federal income tax will "increase considerably as a percent of the family's income."

Fortunately, taxpayers are waking up to this process. They realize what is going on, and they know that it's time for a whole new approach to government. It does little good to try to stop each new spending proposal that comes along; we must strike at the root of the problem by taking away government's ability to increase taxes and spending—and by *slashing* taxes

Around the country, taxpayers are doing this. The movement started, I'm proud to say, in my own state of California. Angered by rising property taxes, the people overwhelmingly passed Proposition 13, which cut property taxes and put severe limits on the state government's taxing authority In the last two years voters in states and localities across the country have followed suit with tax-cut initiatives.

I campaigned for Proposition 13, and I have advocated tax cuts in every state. But we need tax relief at the federal level even more

It should be clear by now that we won't get tax cuts from either a Republican or a Democratic administration. In the last 28 years we've had three Democratic and three Republican Presidents, and taxes have risen steadily under all of them. In the eight years of Dwight Eisenhower's Republican administration, government spending rose from $76 billion to $98 billion, an increase of about 28 percent. In the next eight years under Democratic Presidents John F. Kennedy and Lyndon Johnson, the spending pace picked up a little. With the combined effects of the Vietnam War and the "War on Poverty," federal spending rose from $98 billion to $185 billion, an increase of about 89 percent.

But spending—and taxes—really began to explode under the Republican administrations of Richard Nixon and Gerald Ford. For eight years Nixon and Ford assured us that they were pursuing "fiscally conservative" policies—and the budget rose from $185 billion to $403 billion, an increase of 118 percent. As every taxpayer knows, there's been no relief under the Carter administration. Spending has increased about $213 billion in only three years.

We can see the same trends in the nation's largest state, California. In the last 28 years, California has had two Republican and two Democratic governors. And what has happened to state taxes? Under Republican Governor Goodwin J. Knight, tax revenues increased 38 percent in six years. He was followed by Democrat Pat Brown, widely regarded as a big spender, who increased the state's tax revenues by 104 percent in eight years. Brown was defeated by Ronald Reagan, who criticized the state's excessive spending and promised tax cuts. What happened? Tax revenues skyrocketed 185 percent during Reagan's eight years in office. And recently tax revenues rose 40 percent in the first three years of Jerry Brown's term, before the passage of Proposition 13. Much the same has occurred in New York, Ohio, Illinois, and other states.

The lesson is clear: Under Republican or Democratic administrations, taxes are going to go up. Both the Establishment parties are indebted to special interests, who demand more and more spending on their pet projects. If we want tax cuts, we need a new party—a party of principle, not controlled by

11

special interests. That's why the Libertarian Party was founded and why I'm running for President—to give Americans a real alternative in 1980.

During the course of the 1980 campaign, I'll be detailing a tax plan that will exempt millions of low-income Americans from the income tax entirely, and cut the average American's taxes in half. Under this plan, no one will pay higher taxes, and almost all Americans will find their federal taxes cut dramatically.

At the same time, we must balance the federal budget and stop the binge of deficit spending the federal government has been on for the last twenty years. To that end, in my campaign for governor of California in 1978, I endorsed the National Taxpayers Union drive for a constitutional amendment to balance the federal budget. Polls show that more than 70 percent of the American people support such a measure, and legislatures in 30 states have formally called on Congress to pass a balanced-budget amendment. When four more states pass such a resolution, Congress will be required to pass the amendment or call a constitutional convention for that purpose. I hope that will occur soon; we *need* a balanced federal budget.

Many Establishment economists tell us that there's nothing wrong with deficit spending, that deficits in fact "stimulate the economy" and are good for us. Well, I think all of us know from our personal or business experience that we can't spend more than we take in for very long. An individual or business would go bankrupt very soon. We've had deficits for nineteen of the last twenty years, and we're paying for them now in inflation and unemployment.

When the government spends more than it takes in, it must make up the deficit in one of two ways. It may borrow the money by issuing bonds, which it promises to pay back—out of future tax revenues—at a later date. In this case, the government crowds private borrowers out of the capital market. Because the government is borrowing so much, interest rates rise, and individuals and businesses are unable to borrow money for homes, cars, business expansion, or other purposes. And, of course, taxes must go up in the future to pay off the bonds. So we pay with high interest rates now and high taxes later

The other way to make up the deficit is inflation. Inflation occurs through a process—which the politicians hope we won't understand—called "monetization of the debt." What this impressive-sounding phrase means is that the federal government, with the Federal Reserve System acting as an accomplice before the fact, creates money out of thin air and uses the new dollars to pay its debts. If you or I did that, it would be called counterfeiting; when the government does it, it's "monetary expansion." But the effect is the same—inflation. I'll discuss that more thoroughly in the next chapter.

Deficit spending is no accident—it is a conscious policy by the government and its favored special interests to exploit the American people. The bureaucrats and the special interests get the money borrowed or created—and the rest of us are hurt by high interest rates, higher taxes, and inflation.

This cruel, calculated policy is especially damaging to the poorest members of our society. People living on low or fixed incomes bear the brunt of the high interest rates and inflation. But the bureaucrats and the special interests don't care—they get the benefits and we pay the price. This policy is an outrage, and if we have any compassion for poorer Americans we must put an end to it.

So I think it's clear that Americans are right in demanding a balanced budget. But, it may be argued, President Carter has announced that he is going to balance the budget in 1981. I think it is highly doubtful that we will actually end up with a balanced budget after the smoke has cleared. But even if we do, it's important to ask *how* President Carter intends to balance the budget. And the answer is that he's planning the biggest one-year tax increase in American history. He plans to collect *$90 billion more* in taxes in 1981, over and above the already staggering 1980 tax burden. He's balancing the budget on the backs of the already suffering taxpayers.

This is the *wrong* way to balance the budget—a method designed to help the bureaucrats, not the people. Americans need tax *cuts*, not tax increases.

In my campaign, I'm pledging to balance the federal budget

at a much *lower* level. I want to *reduce* taxes and federal spending. This is the progressive, humane budget policy that America needs for the 1980's. Lower taxes and less government will mean more money for the average American to meet his and his family's needs, more jobs, more productivity, and a higher standard of living for every American

To balance the budget *and* implement a major tax cut, we will have to cut federal spending significantly. Unlike the Establishment politicians who talk in generalities about cutting taxes, but refuse to say where they would cut spending, I am prepared to offer a detailed list of spending cuts.

Billions of dollars can be cut from the budget without any harm to the national interest. Of course, every budget cut will be protested by some special-interest constituency, but it is time to ignore the special interests and cut the budget in the interest of all Americans. We can begin by cutting out programs that serve no useful purpose, programs the government should not be involved in, and programs that do positive harm to our society

Every year the government spends billions of dollars to subsidize favored American businesses. Why should the taxpayers pay these business subsidies? I propose to cut out such boondoggles as the Energy Security Trust Fund, which provides $3.7 billion a year in subsidies to energy companies; the Export-Import Bank, which lends almost $7 billion annually to subsidize American exporting firms, the Foreign Agricultural Service, which spends more than $60 million every year for subsidized research and marketing for agricultural businesses; the Commodity Credit Corporation, which spends more than $3 billion annually to subsidize farmers and keep food prices high; the Maritime Administration, which spends more than $500 million a year to protect the shipping and shipbuilding industries; and dozens of other programs to subsidize businesses at taxpayers' expense. Eliminating these budget items would take a great burden off the taxpayers and make our economy more competitive, more innovative, and more productive. It would mean real free enterprise, rather than the present system of state capitalism.

At the same time that we cut our business subsidies, we

must end the crippling regulations that prevent businesses from producing and limit consumer choices. Such agencies as the Interstate Commerce Commission, the Civil Aeronautics Board, the Federal Trade Commission, the Occupational Safety and Health Administration, and a myriad of others serve no useful purpose. They raise consumer prices, limit our choices, and prevent businesses from responding to consumer demands and creating jobs. Elimination of many of these agencies would save us billions of tax dollars and revitalize our stagnating economy. Workers and consumers would be better protected by competition in a free market, with the courts available to redress injuries or punish fraud, than by bureaucratic regulations. Bureaucrats have no interest in protecting workers and consumers. Their interest is in preserving their own jobs, expanding their bureaucratic empires, collecting a bloated paycheck, and retiring early on a fat pension. Occasionally, they may harass businesses for the sake of publicity, but really protecting the rest of us is the last thing on their mind. Ultimately, they respond to the special interests or their own lust for power, not to the needs of the average American.

Let's get rid of these crippling regulations *and* the business subsidies, and let individuals and businesses interact voluntarily in a free market.

To solve our energy problems, I propose that we eliminate the Department of Energy, a boondoggle that costs us $10 billion a year and serves only to subsidize privileged energy companies and interfere with the production of energy. We can save another $15 billion by eliminating the Department of Education, which centralizes American educational policy, reducing the independence and diversity of schools across the country. I'll have more to say about energy and education in later chapters.

One of the inconsistencies of most politicians who claim to be budget-cutters is military spending. Cut everywhere else, they may say, but don't touch the military. Indeed, this year they are proposing major increases in the military budget. President Carter proposed a $146 billion defense budget, up $16 billion since 1980 and $49 billion since Carter entered office, and Ronald Reagan is demanding even larger increases.

For some reason, people who are very skeptical of most bureaucrats demanding more money for their own departments are nevertheless ready to believe anything the Defense Department says about *its* budget. When it comes to the Pentagon, suddenly "those men in Washington" become "us." I believe we should examine *every* department's budget and refuse to spend money on any program that can't be justified.

We can improve America's national security by redefining our defense objectives and reducing our military budget. We must consider which programs actually defend the United States, and as I will explain in a later chapter, some 60 percent of the military budget in fact goes to defend other countries and support military intervention around the world. This intervention leads to situations like the Iranian crisis, and may even lead to nuclear war. Such a policy is *not* in the best interests of the United States. By cutting the military budget along the lines outlined in Chapter 4, we can save at least $50 billion a year and significantly enhance our national security.

Another target for budget-cutting is the overhead and waste involved in welfare and other transfer programs. I believe we can eliminate much of the fraud and excessive bureaucracy in these programs even without any reduction in payments to really needy recipients.

United Press International reporter Donald Lambro, in his new book *Fat City: How Washington Wastes Your Taxes*, cites estimates by the Government Accounting Office that federal economic-assistance programs are losing $2.5 to $25 billion a year to cheaters and swindlers. GAO experts estimate that $15 billion is the minimum figure. I will see to it that this fraud is eliminated. In addition, I think we can cut down substantially on the number of employees involved in administering these programs. Countless articles written by former government employees attest to the excessive personnel found in every agency. We can reduce the overhead in these programs and effect major savings.

Another area of substantial waste in the government's "antipoverty" program is the granting of contracts to study the poor and the government programs designed to help them. Hundreds of studies, costing as much as $700,000 or more each, have been done on every subject imaginable. Who profits? The bureaucrats who oversee them and the consultants who get the contracts. Economist Thomas Sowell, a professor at UCLA, writes, "To be blunt, the poor are a gold mine. By the time they are studied, advised, experimented with, and administered, the poor have helped many a middle-class liberal to achieve affluence with government money."

This situation is a scandal. It is a rip-off of the American taxpayers, and it does the poor no good at all. In fact, its main effect is to create an entrenched class of affluent, powerful people in and around government who have a vested interest in keeping the poor where they are. I think it's time to put a stop to this outrage.

Finally, we must look at the number and compensation of federal employees. The traditional image of the government employee is the dedicated, underpaid "civil servant." But that picture is far from accurate today. In 1977, the average non-military federal employee made $16,936; the average private-sector worker earned $12,239.

For a graphic demonstration of where our tax dollars really go, consider this: The wealthiest counties in the United States are not Westchester in New York, or DuPage in Illinois, or Marin in California. The two counties with the highest average income in America are Montgomery County, Maryland, and Fairfax County, Virginia—in the suburbs of Washington, D.C. And who lives in these counties? Federal employees, of course, along with the lawyers, lobbyists, and consultants who gravitate toward government like bees toward honey. The entire Washington area, in fact, is the wealthiest metropolitan area in America, indeed, in the world.

The deepening recession may be hurting the rest of us, but not the bureaucrats in Washington. A recent Washington *Post* story was headlined, "This Is a Good Place to Wait While Rest of the Nation Has a Downturn." Bloomingdale's and Neiman-Marcus have recently opened posh new stores in Washington, and the average new home sells for $120,000. *Time* magazine has written that Washington has become "a privileged ghetto, home of a pampered class all but immune to the disheartening tantrums of the economic weather.''

I think it's time to change that. At a time when the American taxpayers are suffering under their tax burden, there are too many federal employees, and their salaries are too high. I propose an immediate *freeze on federal employees and consultants* in those agencies not eliminated. In that way we could reduce the number of federal employees by attrition; as employees leave, they will not be replaced. I'm convinced that there's enough feather-bedding in government that this will not affect any agency's ability to get done whatever legitimate work it has.

Further, I propose an immediate *pay freeze on all federal employees*. As we've seen, federal bureaucrats are as a rule greatly overpaid, and it is time to put a halt to any further pay increases for them. Those federal employees who feel they are then underpaid will be free to resign and take productive jobs in the private sector.

I believe that with measures like these we can cut some $200 billion from the federal budget during my first year in office. And we need not fear that these budget cuts will involve ''sacrifice'' or ''austerity'' for the American people. They will in fact reduce the tax burden, revitalize the economy, create jobs, and begin to reduce the domination of our society by government.

Some may say that these budget cuts are too severe. To those people, I would point out the following: My proposed first-year budget of approximately $425 billion is actually the equivalent of President Kennedy's 1962 budget adjusted for inflation, population growth, and interest on the national debt. That 1962 budget was criticized as excessive at the time. Does anybody believe that the growth of taxes and government since then has improved our lives? I think we'd all be better off with this program of lower taxes and less government spending.

These are some of the cuts I think we can make right away. I would propose them in my first budget. I believe they will lead to tremendous economic growth as the tax and regulatory burdens are lifted from the American people. Businesses will expand and create jobs, consumers will have more money to save or spend, and the economy will grow significantly. As this process occurs, more people will get jobs, and real incomes will increase. Thus many people will be removed from the welfare, food-stamp, unemployment-compensation, and medicaid rolls. We'll be able to make substantial cuts in those programs as the economy improves. The taxpayers will get needed relief, and those currently unable to get jobs will find productive, meaningful employment.

Some rhetorical advocates of tax cuts, like Ronald Reagan, have argued that taxes can be cut without reducing government spending. Reagan supports the Kemp-Roth tax cut, which would be a one-third cut in federal income tax rates phased in over three or four years. He argues that such a tax cut would bring about enough economic growth that there would be no revenue loss to the government. He uses it as an argument *for* Kemp-Roth that government revenues would actually *increase*.

I object to Governor Reagan's proposal on two grounds. In the first place, his tax cut is simply not enough. A 10 percent annual cut in rates, as the Kemp-Roth plan involves, will only cut taxes by the amount that inflation and scheduled Social Security tax increases would otherwise raise them. The average American would not find his tax bill reduced. I think we need a *real* tax cut, not just a rate cut to offset tax increases.

In addition, Governor Reagan seems to believe that total federal spending should not be reduced, since he has defended his program by saying that federal revenues would actually increase. I believe federal spending *should* be reduced. Government is too big and too intrusive, and we must begin to cut it back. We need to get the government off the backs of the American people; slashing the budget and eliminating agencies is a good way to start.

What will be the result of the massive tax and spending cuts that I am proposing? I believe the impact on our society will be extremely positive.

Just consider:

 • Americans will be able to spend more of their own money as they choose.
 • The domination of government over our society will be reduced.

- Millions of new jobs will be created.
- Inflation will be a thing of the past.
- Our standard of living will improve.
- Consumers and businesses will be freed from the regulations, subsidies, and taxes that currently distort the economy, limit consumer choice, and reduce our standard of living.
- Inefficient and wasteful government programs will be eliminated.
- We will begin to remove government from areas where it doesn't belong and to restore government to its proper function of protecting us from harm.
- We will improve the national security of the United States.
- Individual Americans will have more opportunity to make their own decisions.

In short, we will take a giant step toward peace, prosperity, and freedom in America.

CHAPTER 3:

The Inflation Hoax

When Jimmy Carter ran for President in 1976, he regularly criticized President Ford for what he called "the misery index"—the total of the inflation and unemployment rates. In 1976 the misery index stood at 12.5, the sum of an inflation rate of 4.8 percent and an unemployment rate of 7.7 percent.

In March of 1980, after three full years of Jimmy Carter's policies, the misery index had nearly doubled to 24.4, with unemployment at 6.2 percent and inflation soaring to 18.2 percent. The ravages of inflation and unemployment are taking their toll on all Americans.

The consumer price index increased 13.3 percent during 1979, and that figure may have underestimated the price increases in the basic necessities. Using prices in 1967—not that long ago—as 100, by May of 1980 consumer prices had reached 244.9, with no end in sight. Or in other words, the dollar you earned in January, 1979 was worth only 86.7¢ by Christmas. The dollar you earned in 1967 was worth 41.7¢. And the dollar you earned when President Carter took office is now worth only 73¢!

This process has gone on under both Republican and Democratic administrations. In 15½ years of Democratic administrations, the dollar lost 34¢ of its 1948 value. In 16 years of Republican administrations, the value of the dollar declined by 36¢. No matter which party is in power, our dollars steadily lose their value, and our purchasing power is reduced.

Unemployment rates reflect the same dismal story. There were 5,788,000 Americans unemployed in October 1978 and 8,154,000 in May 1980 when the unemployment rate jumped to 7.8 percent of the work force.

Some may argue that at least those Americans who have jobs are not really being hurt by inflation. After all, aren't their wages going up as fast as prices? The answer is no.

According to economist Michael Boskin of Stanford University, the real net spendable earnings of the average American family actually fell by 7.9 percent from spring 1979 to spring 1980. That decline in real income, or purchasing power, was the sharpest in 40 years. And an official government study reported that even families with two people working couldn't keep up with inflation during 1979. According to the Bureau of Labor Statistics, median earnings for two-income families rose 7 percent during the year, compared to the consumer price index rise of 13.3 percent.

Of course, it is probably not necessary to recite these dreary statistics. Most Americans are well aware that their purchasing power is declining as prices soar out of sight. And most of us have grown used to seeing the politicians and their Establishment economists appear on the nightly news and tell us that they don't know what to do about inflation—or that *we* must sacrifice to stop inflation. Well, most of us are already sacrificing, and inflation hasn't stopped.

Conservative politicians tell us greedy labor unions cause inflation. Liberal politicians say that businesses charge too much. President Carter blames the Arabs, a convenient scapegoat since they can't vote in American elections. And they all blame the American consumers, the very people struggling to survive in an inflationary economy.

But inflation is *not* caused by unions, or businesses, or consumers, or the Arabs. Inflation is caused by the federal government, and only the federal government can stop it.

We have to understand first just what inflation is. Inflation, according to the Random House Dictionary, is "an undue expansion or increase of the currency of a country." Rising prices are the result, not the cause, of inflation. Of course, prices are always rising and falling in a free market in response to changing supply and demand. When the supply of oranges is reduced by a Florida snowfall, the price will rise. When demand for housing increases, the price will rise. Conversely, when the supply of a product increases or demand for it decreases, the price will fall. Relative prices of goods change continuously in the free market. If consumers spend more on one product, they must spend less on something else. The reduced demand for other products causes their prices to fall. Thus as some prices rise, others must fall.

Then how can the *general* price level rise? How can we have a situation—like the present—in which the prices of almost all goods and services are rising steadily? This can only happen if there is more money in the economy than before. More money chasing the same amount of goods means that each dollar is worth less. Therefore, it takes more dollars to buy the same product.

How do more dollars get into our economy? Since the dollar is no longer backed by gold or anything else of real value, the federal government and the cartellized banking system face few restrictions on their ability to create money. When the government runs a deficit budget—spends more than it takes in—it has to make up the difference. It does this by borrowing money—by selling bonds and other securities to banks or other buyers. Where do the banks get the money to buy more and more government securities? This is where the mysterious-sounding phrase "monetization of the debt" comes in.

The Federal Reserve Board goes into the open market and buys outstanding government securities from banks and other bondholders. Where does the Fed get the money? Believe it or not, the Fed creates the money *out of thin air* by writing a check on itself. No one had the money before the Fed spent it; it was created with the stroke of a pen. The bank from which the Fed bought the security, of course, now has the new money. It deposits the money in its account at the Fed, increasing its reserves, and then has more money to buy new government securities or lend out. The Fed, which centrally controls the entire banking system, permits the banks in the system to pyramid loans on top of reserves by an eventual multiple of about 6 to 1. That is, if the Fed buys $10 million worth of securities from a bank, increasing its reserves by that amount, the bank can then buy $60 million of new government bonds or other securities. That's called "fractional reserve banking." After each of these transactions there is, say, $100 million more in the nation's money supply than there was an hour ago, but the supply of goods has not increased. So every American's dollars have just decreased in value. This rapid pyramiding of new money created out of thin air—by the Fed and the banks—is what causes inflation.

Professor Murray Rothbard, a member of my Board of Economic Advisors, gives us a telling analogy:

> Suppose, for example, that the Angel Gabriel descended upon us tonight and magically, overnight, doubled everyone's stock of money, of dollars, doubled everyone's bank account, money in purse or wallet, or under the floorboards. What would happen the next morning? Everyone would *think* himself twice as well off, would bless the Angel Gabriel, and rush out to spend the new money. But the stock of capital equipment, of resources and goods and services in the economy, would not have changed. So, while the supply of goods and services remained the same, the doubled supply of dollars would quickly bid all prices to roughly twice the height that they were before the bonanza. As a whole, we would be no better off. Except: that those people who rushed out early in the morning to spend the cash would benefit, while those who waited until prices rose, would lose out during this interim period.

Who benefits from this process? The government, of course. Just as you or I would benefit if we could legally print money, so the government benefits from creating money for itself. The difference is that if you or I did it, it would be called counterfeiting; when the government does it, it's called "monetary policy."

But there are other people who benefit as well, and that explains why the political process always produces inflation. The people who benefit are those who get the new money first, before it circulates through the economy and raises all prices. Defense contractors, other companies who do business with the government, government employees, consultants, and the other special interests who cluster around the public trough all benefit from inflation and don't really want to see it stopped. When the government creates new money, it goes to these people first. They spend the money while prices are still at their previous levels; then, as prices begin to rise in response to this new money, the rest of us find *our* dollars will buy less. The result is that there is a massive transfer of buying power from the American people to those special interests with access to government money. Middle class and poor Americans end up subsidizing Chrysler, Lockheed, and high-paid government bureaucrats and consultants.

Another particularly insidious and all-too-familiar effect of inflation is the "promotion" of American taxpayers into higher and higher tax brackets, so that a higher percentage of their income is taken by the government. For example, assume that a taxpayer makes a gross income of $20,000 this year and has $5,000 worth of deductions. The federal income tax he pays on the remaining $15,000 is $2,352. Now assume that he is lucky enough to make enough money next year to match the 18 percent rate of inflation in the first quarter of 1980. His income would now be $23,600. Assume his deductions also increase by 18 percent, to $5,900. His taxable income is now $17,700—which buys no more than this year's $15,000—but the tax he pays increases to $3,123, an increase of 33 percent.

Even if you adjust the tax for inflation, the government has ripped him off for $348—and he's one of the lucky ones, whose gross income has actually kept pace with inflation. Generally, for every 1 percent increase in inflation, taxes rise by 1.6 percent—giving the government another incentive to keep inflating.

Another problem caused by inflation is the "boom and bust" cycle of inflation and unemployment. Government manipulation of the supply of money and credit leads to a distortion of interest rates for businesses. Inflationary credit creation by the Federal Reserve System makes new funds available for business expansion without a corresponding voluntary act of saving by investors and consumers. The ratio of consumption to savings is distorted from its "equilibrium" or free market level.

To businesspeople, the new funds seem to be genuine investments. But unlike free market investments, these funds do not arise from voluntary savings. The new money is invested by businessmen in various projects and paid out to workers

25

and suppliers as higher wages and prices. But much of the money is invested in the production of goods for which the real market is much less than the government interventions made it appear.

As the new money filters down to the whole economy, consumers receiving it as wages do not spend it in the way businesses expected. Many investments are then revealed to be wasteful and not based on real consumer preferences. When this happens, businesses fail, plants close, and workers lose their employment—forced from their jobs by the machinations of the Federal Reserve. In this way inflation always leads to unemployment; and when we stop inflation, we'll greatly reduce our unemployment problem as well.

Professor F. A. Hayek, the Nobel Prize-winning economist, wrote about this in his recent article *Unemployment: Inevitable Consequence of Inflation*. In his words,

> Inflation, has, of course, many other bad effects, much more grave and painful than is realized by most people who have not lived through a serious inflation. But the effect that is most devastating, and at the same time the least understood, is that in the long run inflation invariably produces extensive unemployment. . . . We do not have the choice between inflation and unemployment, just as we cannot choose between overeating and indigestion: Overeating may be very pleasant while we are doing it, but the day of reckoning—the indigestion—is sure to follow.

To reduce unemployment, we *must* stop inflation. Any other "solution" to unemployment is just a quick fix that won't address the real problem.

Many readers will note that in early 1980 interest rates were soaring and that investment capital has been difficult to get for many businesses. This is because interest rates reflect the fact that banks and other loan making institutions expect inflation to continue. After years of bipartisan inflation of the money supply, lenders have come to expect that the money creating process will continue. This means that next year's dollars will be worth less than this year's. As a result, lenders will require higher interest payments to offset the fact that each dollar received in the future to pay off a loan will be worth less. Higher and higher interest rates are the result, not the cause, of greater and greater inflation.

Inflation is now perceived by most Americans as a fact of life; it seems to be just a question of how much and how fast. Understandably, people have no confidence in the ability of the President, or Congress, or the Democratic party, or the Republican Party to control inflation.

If you look at the other contenders for President, you would have no reason to be confident. Jimmy Carter can be described as an expert on inflation, he's created so much of it in such a short time. Inflation has soared from 4.8 percent to 18 percent in the last three years. And Carter has no program to stop inflation. His latest idea is to increase spending for the Council on Wage and Price Stability from $10 million to $25 million—higher spending to reduce inflation! But the wage and price "guidelines" enforced by COWPS are a farce, though they've done less damage than a return to actual controls. Carter promised to balance the budget, but he didn't. Even the 1981 budget will not really be balanced if we count all federal expenditures. Now Carter is trying to stop inflation by plunging us into a recession, but he hasn't dealt with the real cause of inflation—the expansion of the money supply.

John Anderson's solution is that we all must sacrifice. I reject any solution which requires the *victims* of current government policies to suffer even more. Anderson has proposed to levy higher taxes on companies that give their employees wage increases to keep up with inflation. And he has said he might support a government-imposed "freeze" on wages and prices. Wage and price controls failed when Richard Nixon imposed them (and Anderson supported them) and they would fail again. Anderson's outspoken advocacy of government-imposed "solutions" and his opposition to a general tax cut hardly demonstrate any profound "difference." Rather, they show a basic devotion to the very way of thinking that created the problem in the first place.

Ronald Reagan's rhetoric stops well short of identifying the real solutions to inflation, and his record as Governor of California should give us no hope that he might stop inflation. Today he is promising to cut taxes and limit government spending. He made the same promises when he ran for Governor of California; but in eight years he doubled state spending, instituted a withholding tax, and shifted the tax burden from one sector of society to another as if other people's money was a pea in a giant shell game. Today, while he vaguely calls for reduced spending, he can't resist promising *increased* spending in a number of areas—military programs, subsidies to the arts, urban jobs programs, aid to Chrysler, and on and on. Once again, as we noted in Chapter Two, there is always more political pressure to *increase* spending in any specific area than to decrease it. Like all politicians, Ronald Reagan promises "overall" spending cuts, but his specific promises are all for spending increases. A Reagan administration with spending programs such as he's promised would have to keep inflating to pay for its spending.

Does all this mean that there is no solution to inflation? Does any presidential candidate have a real answer?

There *is* a way to stop inflation, a Libertarian solution which is workable for the 1980's. What would a Libertarian administration do to stop inflation in this decade?

First, my federal budget for fiscal 1981 would be balanced, and so would every budget thereafter. This will eliminate the deficits which provoke the creation of so much worthless money. I would veto any legislation which would exceed the expenditure level of these budgets. And each succeeding budget will be balanced at lower and lower levels of taxing and spending, restoring hundreds of billions of dollars per year to the market economy. This will stimulate savings, investment, and productivity—which will create more jobs, goods, and services.

Second, I would seek to establish a sound backing for United States currency, probably by restoring the gold standard, and to have our currency freely convertible into gold. At the present price of gold, the United States owns enough gold to redeem every cent of money now in circulation. In doing this we would be following the advice of a long line of great Americans like

Thomas Paine, Thomas Jefferson, and Andrew Jackson, who believed that gold was the "people's money"—the average person's protection against the government's debasement of the currency. Jackson said in 1834, "We must end the power of the 'Paper Aristocracy' to use paper money to enrich itself at the expense of the humble members of society—the farmers, mechanics, and laborers—who have neither the time nor the means of securing like favors to themselves." When our dollars are worth something, when we have confidence in our money, we will have won a major battle against those who cheapen our money and then point the finger of blame at us.

Finally, I would strike at the root of inflation by directing a stop to the increase in the money supply. I would appoint to the Federal Reserve Board new members who will resist the political pressures to inflate. The single most important step that can be taken to end inflation is that the Federal Reserve must cease purchasing new assets, such as Treasury bonds, on the open market. The purchase of assets by the Fed means the creation of money out of thin air. My appointees to the Fed's Board of Governors would end this practice, thus taking a giant step toward a stable money supply and an end to rising prices.

Ultimately, however, there is no reason for fourteen men—the Fed's Board of Governors—to hold the economic fate of 220 million Americans in their hands. The Fed was created by New York banking interests, and its main purpose is to make the banking industry a privileged cartel not subject to the normal rules of competition in the marketplace. Its decisions are political ones, made in the interest of the political and financial Establishments. It allows the major banks to create huge amounts of money for their own benefit. And as Yale Professor Edward Tufte has demonstrated in his book, *Political Control of the Economy*, the Fed always increases the money supply just before a presidential election, giving voters the illusion of prosperity.

Sherman Maisel, a governor of the Federal Reserve from 1965 to 1972, wrote of the 1972 election campaign that, "It was . . . clear to the White House where new expansionary pressures ought to be generated. The finger pointed right at the Federal Reserve. Because of the independent position of the Fed, no direct orders could be issued, but the White House made its views plain. . . . If an election were to be won [in 1972], the Federal Reserve would have to increase the money supply at far more than the 4.2 percent average of 1969-70.'' What happened? The Fed did accelerate the growth of money in 1971-72, as the Nixon administration wanted. And, Tufte writes, the 1972 election was nothing special in this respect. The money supply is almost always increased more rapidly just before a presidential election.

The result of this is that the economy seems to be improving at election time. The new money encourages businesses to expand, hire more workers, and raise wages. Voters get the illusion of prosperity. But after the election, when the rate of expansion of the money supply falls off, businesses find that the prosperity was only an illusion. There isn't really enough new consumer demand to sustain the investments. Businesses fail, workers lose their jobs, a recession results—but the election is over, so the politicians don't care.

We can limit these schemes through such institutional arrangements as a balanced budget and the appointment of Fed Governors who will end the expansion of the money supply. But we can not let our economic fate depend on the appointment of ''good people'' to the Fed. To stop inflation, allow our economy to work smoothly, and preserve our liberty, we must eliminate the Federal Reserve. The Fed's only functions are to protect the privileged banking industry and inflate the money supply. The American people would be better off without this agency.

We should also carefully consider the recommendations of Nobel Laureate F. A. Hayek with regard to our monetary system. After studying monetary policy for some fifty years, Professor Hayek has recently suggested that competition would benefit consumers in the provision of money as it does in all other areas. He recommends repealing legal tender laws and allowing businesses and consumers to use whatever kind of money they choose. Thus, he argues, if a buyer and seller wished to use gold, Swiss francs, or whatever to transact business, they should be free to do so. This would allow them to make contracts in a stable form of money and partially escape the effects of government-caused inflation. Hayek believes that such a policy would help to protect individuals from inflation and act as a check on the government's desire to inflate. Professor Hayek has offered us a potentially very important proposal for removing our money supply from political control. We should give it serious consideration.

These steps—a balanced budget, sound money, and an end to expansion of the money supply—might be described as radical. They will be opposed by the politicians, the Establishment economists, and the bureaucrats—the same people who, through their systematic denial of economic reality and their use of our monetary system in their own interests, have brought us inflation, unemployment, recessions, and now "stagflation." But what is the alternative? How long will we, the American people, put up with 8 or 10 or 13 or 20 percent inflation? And we must remember that inflation will not long remain in this range. Political pressure is always directed toward increasing the rate of inflation until we reach hyperinflation—inflation running at 100 percent, then 1000 percent, soon racing so fast that it can't be calculated. This has happened many times in world history—in Germany in the 1920's, for example, when workers demanded to be paid twice a day because their money lost value by the hour, or in several South American countries recently, where the whole society was torn apart by the ravages of hyper-inflation. It *can* happen here if we don't take the necessary steps now to *stop* inflation. We cannot be satisfied with candidates whose only solution to inflation is to slow down the rate of *increase* of inflation.

We deserve better than that. We deserve a sound currency that has real value. We deserve substantial, immediate relief from government's practice of spending more than it takes in and making up the difference through the creation of worthless money. We deserve an immediate end to the practice which government calls "monetary policy," but which you and I would call counterfeiting.

We *can* stop inflation. And when we do, we will have accomplished a major part of our goal of revitalizing our economy and improving our standard of living. We can free our-

31

selves from the boom-and-bust cycle of inflation, depression, and unemployment. Americans who live on fixed incomes will no longer find their incomes slipping below the poverty level. Middle-class Americans will no longer see their buying power shrinking every month. Businesses will be able to make accurate investment decisions, reducing the incidence of business failures and unemployment. Our dollar would be worth a dollar, and Americans would once more look to the future with hope, rather than doubt and the premonition of disaster. Ending inflation would do more to cure our national "malaise" than any number of hypocritical speeches by those who keep the inflation-machine running.

CHAPTER 4:

Non-Intervention: The Key to Peace

All of us are used to hearing politicians trumpet the need for "new ideas," especially around election time. But in the area of foreign policy, there has not been a truly new idea offered within the lifetime of any person now 30 years old. For decades now, the policy pursued by Democrats and Republicans alike—the "bipartisan foreign policy"—has been one of perpetual global involvement, with the occasional, inevitable wars such a posture entails. What does this course promise for the future? All indications are that a war in the area of the Persian Gulf is more than likely. Other wars—in Central or South America, in Korea again—are entirely possible. The spending of at least *$2 trillion* for defense over the next *decade* is certain. Here there are no "new ideas" offered at all, but merely a drifting along the path we have traveled for many years.

The situation is now so bleak that twice in the period following the Soviet invasion of Afghanistan, the Carter administration leaked word to the press that it would consider using nuclear weapons if the Soviets moved into Pakistan or Iran. President Carter is beginning to mobilize a Rapid Deployment Force, capable of being moved into any trouble spot on earth at a moment's notice. He is also adding bases around the Middle East, moving toward a reinstitution of the draft, and pushing through Congress great increases in military spending—thus mocking the Democratic platform of 1976 and his own election promises.

Meanwhile, the Republican Party has been totally captured by the hawks. (Even "moderate" George Bush spoke during his campaign of our "survivability" in an all-out nuclear war.) Ronald Reagan earnestly urges us to return with him to the Golden Years of the Cold War; his response to Soviet aggression in Afghanistan would be to blockade Cuba, perhaps send missiles to the Afghan rebels, and give the Pentagon everything it wants (literally) in the way of new weapons systems—the better to confront the Russians in the years to come.

As for "independent" John Anderson, he supports, among other things, a strong U.S. naval presence in the Persian Gulf, the Arabian Sea, and the northern Indian Ocean; increased military aid to Pakistan's dictator, General Zia; and the introduction of theater nuclear weapons into Europe. As in so many other areas, when we go beyond the "image" and examine Anderson's foreign policy views closely, it turns out that he stands about two and a half centimeters distant from his Republican and Democratic opponents.

Thus, the policies of Democrat Carter, Republican Reagan, and erstwhile Republican Anderson in foreign affairs promise us more of the same: a new arms race and stepped-up intervention in the affairs of other countries. But it is an old and wise saying, "By their fruits ye shall know them." What have been the results of our policy of global interventionism which our political leaders are so eager to continue *ad infinitum*? Have they proved to be so uniformly brilliant as to place that policy beyond question or debate?

The worst result—so far—of that bipartisan policy was the Vietnam War. In this campaign year, the silence that the major party candidates have maintained on that war, just a few years after the fall of Saigon, is passing strange, is it not? Fifty thousand American dead, hundreds of thousands more maimed in body or spirit, millions of Indochinese caught up and destroyed by the war, our society rocked by turmoil and near-insurrection—it's as if none of this had ever happened. Is this the kind of "responsibility" we should expect from those who represent old and established parties in this country—that the war that seared the mind of a whole generation should vanish from public discussion like a dream? Have we really understood the whole lesson of that awful war? Or is it possible that the blackout on thinking about the recent past in Vietnam is linked to the plans our leaders have to risk a rerun in the near future?

But Vietnam was only the most extreme instance—and the

logical culmination—of our prevailing system in foreign affairs. We have attempted to manipulate foreign peoples throughout the world, promoting governments "friendly" to undefined "American interests," rather than allowing people to form their own. In the name of "free enterprise" we have propped up dictators who are "anti-Communist," while these dictatorial regimes, and our support of them, are the greatest single factor *undermining* the credibility of capitalism throughout the Third World. We have actively intervened, through diplomatic, economic, and military means, to protect American business interests abroad, instead of pursuing a policy of free trade and noninterference that would allow firms to invest in other nations *at their own risk*. We have used American arms, troops, covert operations by the CIA, the management of international trade, and a host of other methods to try to shape world events to our liking.

And we have failed. Throughout large portions of the world we are hated. Iran is perhaps the classic case of the failure of our interventionist policy. Americans sit puzzled and angry in front of their TV sets, unable to make any sense out of the spectacle of Iranian mobs shouting "Death to the United States!" Yet there is much to learn from the events in Iran in the past year and a half, if we have the courage to learn it. We must go beyond a condemnation—altogether justified—of the seizure of the hostages. What we need is a little knowledge of what President Carter dismisses as "ancient history"—that is, the history of our relations with Iran over the past few decades, up to and including the first two years of Carter's own administration.

Twice over the past forty years, the United States was instrumental in changing the government of Iran, much to the displeasure of the Iranian people. In 1941, we worked with the British and Russians to overthrow the then shah, and install the young Mohammed Reza Pahlavi—"our" shah—in power. In 1953, when a nationalist movement led by Mohammed Mossadegh threatened to send the autocratic and corrupt shah into exile, the CIA engineered a coup to overthrow Mossadegh and re-establish the shah on his throne. Perhaps by coincidence, control of Iranian oil passed from British to American hands.

For the next 25 years, we sent the shah money and advisors—technocrats from elite American universities—to "modernize" Iran, which meant the demolition of the traditional Iranian way of life. The Pahlavi dynasty imposed central planning on Iran's economy, harming the merchants of the bazaar and the productive middle class; seized huge tracts of land, later giving back some of it in a sanctimonious gesture; imposed more and higher taxes; and generally treated Iran like its own private preserve. The wealth of the country was squandered on an attempt to make Iran into a military superpower, the regional policeman of the Persian Gulf. And when the people of Iran grumbled at this disruption and despoiling of their lives, the CIA helped set up SAVAK, the shah's secret police, which terrorized, through torture and murder, anyone who dissented from his rule.

Through all these years, the Iranian people heard their tyrant adulated by the spokesmen for American democracy. As the shah's twin sister, Ashraf Pahlavi, has boasted: "It is a matter of record that America's leaders have publicly praised and supported the shah's regime for almost four decades"; these leaders include "the last eight American presidents." She might have added that, in all that time, U.S. support of the shah's dictatorship elicited not a peep—"courageous" or otherwise—from Congressman Anderson; and that, until the Shah's death, Ronald Reagan called him "as good an ally as we've ever had," and had offered to testify to his moral character before any international tribunal.

Despite this record of insolent intervention in Iranian affairs, President Carter purports to be bewildered by Iranian demands that we apologize for past misconduct and pledge to steer clear of involvement in their domestic politics in the future. Similarly, Richard V. Allen, Ronald Reagan's chief advisor on foreign policy, who visited Tehran five years ago, admits that "below the top levels of government I found nothing but contempt and scorn for Americans," but claims he's at a complete loss to explain such hostility.

What is truly surprising is that our political leaders would evidence such surprise. All they need do to understand the feelings of Iranians is to put themselves in their place. The Iranians are at least as patriotic and nationalistic a people as the Americans, and their national pride has been painfully bruised by decades of foreign domination. Vast numbers of Iranians have harbored for us much the same sentiments that Poles and Hungarians are reported to cherish for *their* Russian "allies." These feelings of hatred and resentment we have become all too familiar with in recent years. They are the natural fruit of our policy of intervention, and they will continue to grow as long as that policy persists.

At this point, I must become "defensive" for a moment—to forestall an accusation which might arise in the mind of the reader.

Often when someone strongly criticizes the foreign policy of Democratic and Republican administrations, as I have been doing—when he points out that our support of dictators like Pahlavi in Iran, Somoza in Nicaragua, Trujillo in the Dominican Republic, and Pinochet in Chile—might have something to do with the hostility against our country in various parts of the world—then that critic is attacked as "anti-American." But I should like to know when American patriotism began to entail, not only love for our own free and productive people, but also for the parasitic elites around the world kept in existence by their armies and their secret police? Just when was that blood-brotherhood sworn between Americans and the foreign exploiters of the sort that has existed from time immemorial—and against which the American Revolution was itself an uprising? If we want to apply the term "anti-American" here, then it should be attached not to the critics of our bipartisan foreign policy—but to those who have enthusiastically placed the good name of the United States behind countless political gangsters in every part of the world.

So, far from being "anti-American," it is the Libertarian foreign policy that is the much older tradition in our nation. That policy is based on the principle of defending the United States and avoiding political involvement in the affairs of other countries. Like so much else in our approach, it derives from the American Revolution and the founding fathers.

It used to be much better known than it is today that the founders of the United States had in mind a very definite foreign policy for the new republic. It was called "neutrality," or, as we would now say, "nonintervention." The classic expressions of this position are by George Washington and Thomas Jefferson. As Washington put it, in his Farewell Address, "The Great rule in conduct for us, in regard to foreign Nations, is in extending our commercial relations to have with them as little political connection as possible." And Jefferson's statement, in his First Inaugural Address, is even more succinct: "Peace, commerce, and honest friendship with all nations—entangling alliances with none."

It is important to understand that these statements were not merely offered as good advice and common sense by men with wide knowledge of international affairs. Rather, they were part and parcel of the whole philosophy of government that the founders bequeathed to us. In their system, a meddling foreign policy was to be condemned above all because it would eventually destroy the kind of government that we had established here.

In the Inaugural Address cited above, Jefferson outlines the blessings enjoyed by Americans—the abundant resources of the land, the character of the citizenry—and then asks: "What more is necessary to make us a happy and prosperous people?" His reply is a good short statement of the Libertarian approach:

> Still one thing more, fellow citizens—a wise and frugal government, which shall restrain men from injuring one another, which shall leave them otherwise free to regulate their own pursuits of industry and improvement, and shall not take from the mouth of labor the bread it has earned. This is the sum of good government, and this is necessary to close the circle of our felicity.

Note the insistence on *frugal* government. Washington had also insisted on it in his Farewell Address, when he warned against the perils of a vast national debt, whose burdens could only be forestalled by "avoiding occasions of expense by cultivating peace."

The policy of intervention, entangling alliances and war, the founders were convinced, would bring about a massive, expensive, and debt-ridden government, resembling those of the Old World to which our new and shining republic now stood in stark contrast. There were many differences between our nation and the empires of Europe, but this was the most important: *They* were military machines, dedicated to the restless search for national power and glory. *Ours* was consecrated to a different end: the preservation of the rights to life, liberty, and the pursuit of happiness of individual men and women. Just as a foreign policy of intervention, imperialism, and war was natural to the European powers—it was what they were all *about*—so one of nonintervention, respect for other peoples, and peace was natural to our republic.

That this was, indeed, the basic philosophy of the founding fathers will not be contradicted by many. But the conventional wisdom has it that while it may have fitted the circumstances of the year 1800, it is totally irrelevant to the complex and interrelated world of 1980. This is a dogma that has been enunciated so often and from so many political pulpits, that it can be said to be the knee-jerk response whenever the idea of nonintervention is brought up.

And yet the same people who say that our complicated modern world has made neutrality obsolete never say, for instance, that the Bill of Rights is now a quaint little period-piece. Obviously that wouldn't be true. On the contrary—the newer and more sophisticated threats to individual liberty that modern government can mount have made the principles embedded in the Bill of Rights all the *more* precious. And the Bill of Rights derives from the same men and the milieu that passed on to us the doctrine of nonintervention.

Those men knew what they were doing. Whatever may be said of the founding fathers, there is one fact that no one will dispute: they had a rather good idea of what would be required to maintain the political system they had created. They understood that the balanced system of limited government they had established was a delicate thing, unprecedented in history, and that a course of constant war and preparation for war would have the inevitable tendency to undermine it. A "vigorous"

39

foreign policy would dangerously shift power away from the citizen and toward the government, and, within the government itself, toward the executive branch and the office of the President, who, in time, would come to resemble a king or a Caesar.

We, who lived through the Vietnam War, have reason to know the truth of this view. What we saw then were intelligence agencies spying on our citizens and even systematically breaking the law; the beating and imprisonment of dissenters; the people deceived by their leaders; and Congress turned into a rubber-stamp for far-reaching schemes hatched by a few men in the executive branch.

But the connection between war and the massive government we see today runs even deeper than that, as modern scholars have shown. Professor Jonathan Hughes of Northwestern University, for instance, has studied the growth of government power in the United States in his book, *The Governmental Habit*. He finds a direct relationship between the wars the United States has fought in this century and the growth of the federal Leviathan so bemoaned by American conservatives. Starting back in World War I, he states, "National emergency became the catch-all justification for the extension of federal power into the private economy," and that power expanded with each such emergency. Above all, with each new war, the flood of government spending grew ever stronger: "Once expanded by the fiscal force of war expenditures, the size of government, measured by spending outlays, did not then contract back to pre-war levels . . . Each war inflated the economy and gave the federal spending mechanism a scope it did not previously have." In other words, each time it was a case of two steps forward and one step back for the power of government. With one exception—Vietnam, where the end of the war brought *no* reduction of government expenditures.

To those who fear Big Government, I would point out that nothing nourishes Big Government as much as war. And I would respectfully ask the friends of free enterprise just how much they suppose will be left of our free market system and of the principle of private property after another generation or two of war and preparation for war?

40

Other scholars have investigated the effects of our interventionist policy on the productivity of the American economy. Professor Seymour Melman of Columbia University has found that the spending of hundreds of billions of dollars by the Defense Department decade after decade has fundamentally transformed our economic system. More and more, the economic scene is coming to be dominated by the firms that form part of the Pentagon network of thousands of industrial enterprises. "A new kind of enterprise has become characteristic of military industry," Professor Melman writes, one quite different from the typical enterprise in a competitive capitalist economy. "This firm *maximizes* cost and *maximizes* subsidies from the state management."

> It can draw on the federal budget for virtually unlimited capital. It operates in an insulated monopoly market that makes the state-capitalist firms, singly and jointly, impervious to inflation, to poor productivity performance, to poor product design, and poor production management. . . . That is the state-capitalist replacement for the classic self-correcting mechanisms of the competitive, cost-minimizing, profit-maximizing firm.

The deterioration of our productive capacity caused by trillions of dollars of unproductive military outlays since 1946 has been slow but relentless. As Professor Melman puts it, "Unseen, for example, was the fact that while the stock of missiles was enlarged and renewed, the railroad rolling stock deteriorated without replacement." When the proportion of our national income going to the military is significantly greater than that of Germany or Japan, is it any wonder that our industries, starved for capital, have fallen far behind theirs? The fight to slash the Pentagon's budget is the fight to preserve what is left of our free market economy.

Thus, the damage inflicted on us by what President Eisenhower called "the military-industrial complex" has not only affected our political system, but our economic system as well. The fact is that *not even America* ever was rich enough to sustain the burdens of empire.

What is the reason we are being asked to acquiesce in the undermining of our freedom and prosperity? What are the urgent grounds that require the continued collectivization and militarization of our society? The answer is, of course, the Communist Threat. Or, more precisely—since the People's Republic of China is now our "friend"—the Soviet Threat. But to believe that any danger the Soviet Union poses for us demands an American policy of intervention—as distinguished from a policy of the strongest necessary defense of the United States itself—is to radically misunderstand the world situation.

If the United States cannot control the world, how much less can the Soviet Union do so? When all is said and done, the Soviet Union is a semi-developed country, incapable even of adequately feeding itself, even though a hugh proportion of its population is engaged in agriculture. Soon ethnic Russians will constitute less than half of the inhabitants of the USSR. It is surrounded by apathetic or openly or covertly hostile Communist states—on the longest border in the world it has as an enemy the most heavily populated nation in the world, a nation comprising one-quarter of the human race. Four of the five countries with nuclear missiles have those missiles trained on Russian cities. And to the degree that cultural and economic contacts with the West have increased, the more courageous of the Soviet citizens have begun to dissent from the policies of their government and agitate for change.

Above all, the Soviets are the victims of an utterly wrongheaded economic system, the product of perversely mistaken ideas. While the increasing complexity of technology and of economic life demands a *decentralized* system, ruled by the market and based on private property and individual initiative, the Russians cling to obsolete notions of government ownership and central economic "planning." Their only hope for improvement lies in greater reliance on market mechanisms, such as have been instituted in Hungary and, of course, Yugoslavia. But this necessary evolution—which tends to bring with it a relaxation of political controls, as well—could only take place in the context of international calm and détente. An atmosphere of confrontation and challenge is likely to wreck any prospects for it.

It is onto this vast country, wracked with economic, political, and ethnic problems, that we project the fantasy-qualities of near omnipotence and endless patient cunning—a sort of Caucasian version of Fu Manchu. The *reductio ad absurdum* of this notion, as of so much else, can be found in the views of Ronald Reagan, who has admonished us in these terms: "Let's not delude ourselves. The Soviet Union underlies all the unrest that is going on. If they weren't engaged in this game of dominoes, there wouldn't be any hot spots in the world." Reagan's view, that we are "in a poker game with the Soviet Union," is, with some nuances of differences, shared by Carter and Anderson as well.

It is no secret that well-financed groups recently have heated up Cold War propaganda to a new high point. Bizarre scenarios of future Soviet actions abound, adding to the hysteria in Washington. Some of our more excitable Cold Warriors picture a sudden Soviet sweep to snatch up Western Europe. This must occasion a good deal of mirthless laughter in the Kremlin, since Russia needs a united, Communist Germany on its periphery about as much as it needs another China; moreover, what with trying to control the Poles and Rumanians, it is not likely to welcome the challenge of trying to keep the French in line.

Another imminent threat some people like to paint for us is of a surprise Soviet attack that will simultaneously destroy all, or virtually all, of the U.S. nuclear forces. The Russians, we are told, will then be in a position to dictate their demands to the President of the United States over the hotline. Considering that the most technologically sophisticated nation in the world was not able to lift two aircraft out of the desert (in the absence of any enemy forces) without having them crash into each other, the Soviets would have to possess a truly imbecilic faith in their own flawless expertise in order to entertain the suggested "plan." The world situation is disturbing enough without lobbyists for a blank check to the Pentagon bothering us with their nightmares.

Does this mean that the Soviet Union poses no conceivable threat to the United States? No. But whatever danger may exist should be kept in perspective. For them, as for us and all other

43

peoples, peace is the indispensable condition for *any* kind of future. The Soviets are extremely proud of the "achievements" of socialism (such as they are); they realize that nuclear war would wipe out those achievements and set them back many generations, if they survived at all.

Let us remember that it was not so very long ago that Communist China—now amicably known as the People's Republic of China—was the great, impending menace, a threat so palpable that we had to undertake two land wars in Asia to thwart it. Now, of course, it is practically an *ally*, which we are being asked from many quarters to help arm. This suggests that international politics is a much less simple matter than the paranoid scenario of a single, ruthless clique bent on "world conquest."

As far as any conflict short of nuclear war is concerned, the ironic fact is that if history proves anything it is that war *promotes* the spread of Communism. As William Shawcross, an authority on the subject, wrote of the Khmer Rouge (Cambodian Communists):

> They had no hope of winning power whatsoever; it was only the destruction of the 1970-75 war, which ruined Cambodian society, that enabled them to seize the country and impose their terrible will upon it. Just as the Bolsheviks could not have taken Russia but for the dislocation caused by the First World War, so the Khmer Rouge grew on the chaos of the 1970-75 war.

This was, of course, the war brought to Cambodia by Richard Nixon and Henry Kissenger. It's easy to guess how many of the anti-Communist regimes in the Persian Gulf area are likely to survive a war there. This is doubtless a major reason why all of those regimes are anxious to keep the region free of any super-power involvement—including ours.

How then do the tried and proven principles of nonintervention apply to our present position in the world?

A new approach to our foreign policy must begin with the question, What is our foreign policy supposed to *do*? Will we remain the world's policeman forever, generating animosity, bankrupting ourselves, and altering our society to fit a role we were never meant to fill? Or should our focus be on *the defense of the United States*?

I believe that our foreign policy and defense spending should be limited to protecting the United States from attack or invasion, and that, to do this properly, we must disengage from other commitments. This would not only allow us to make drastic cuts in our defense spending, and limit our involvement in conflicts around the world; it would actually make us *more secure*. For the fact is that more than 60 percent of the Pentagon's budget today goes for the defense not of the United States, but of other countries, from Western Europe, to the Middle East, to South Korea and Japan. Not only are these nations covered by the American "nuclear umbrella," but we are spending billions on troop deployments, military bases, gifts of armaments, security commitments, mutual defense treaties, repressive police technologies, and the buttressing of proxy regimes. When we combine this direct spending with the costs of so-called back-up forces designed for our participation in future wars in Europe, the Middle East, or East Asia, it becomes quite clear that our principal focus is now far removed from the security of our own country against foreign attack or invasion.

We should disengage from our commitments to defend Japan and South Korea, and stop subsidizing their defense. We now spend nearly $25 billion each year to defend those nations, which are perfectly capable of defending themselves. Japan, in particular, is one of the most economically healthy and powerful countries in the world; this is not totally divorced from the fact that it spends less than 1 percent of its Gross National Product on the military, while our military budget amounts to more than 6 percent of our GNP.

The same solution holds for Western Europe. Today we are spending nearly $83 billion a year on the defense of our NATO allies, at a time when our economic performance compares rather unfavorably with that of some Western European nations. Western Europe is more than capable of defending itself against the Soviet Union. Its population is greater than that of the Warsaw Pact countries, and it has not only twice their

GNP, but a much greater technological sophistication. Why cannot we see the wisdom in the challenge of Michel Jobert, former foreign minister of France: "Is the United States resolutely ready to convince its allies that they must defend themselves—much as France was able to do after a solitary effort—instead of encouraging them to brood sadly under the leaky American atomic umbrella?" This is after all the year 1980, not 1945.

One thing that a Libertarian defense policy most definitely entails is that there must be no draft. The doctrine that the state has a kind of right of eminent domain over your body reaches its ultimate, logical conclusion in the draft. Twist and turn the matter as one may, I can see no way of refuting the fact that the draft is simply a form of involuntary servitude—which is to say, a form of slavery. It can have no place, at any time, in a free society.

There would be no question of the draft if it were not for our present interventionist foreign policy. The manpower required for the defense of the United States could be met by a volunteer system with great ease. This is likely to cost more than a system of conscription. But just as there can be no question of drafting secretaries to work for the Pentagon, or—shall we say?—commandeering the aircraft and other weapons from manufacturers, so there should be no question of corralling young men—or women—by force into the armed service. Young people, like all of us, did not obtain the rights to their lives and liberty by grant of government; they hold them as inalienable rights. A government that would try to draft them would be no better than a kidnapper.

Since the draft is out of the question in any free society worthy of the name, there is no point in draft registration. And if the draft is unacceptable, so, clearly, is any "national service" scheme, that would compel young people to spend time working—for a remuneration decided by the government—on one or another project designated as worthy and character-building by our political leaders. National service, like the draft itself, is the ultimate in victimless crime legislation. The "crime" is turning eighteen; the penalty is two years at hard labor. Why, I wonder, are there so many people in Washington

46

anxious to help remake our country in the image of the discredited fascist societies of the past, or the foundering Communist societies of the present?

Does all this mean that Libertarians are "isolationists"? By no means. Like our classical liberal forebears, Libertarians are *cosmopolitans*. We look forward to a world bound together by peaceful international trade—a state of affairs that political involvements can only hinder. Let me cite the statements of Jefferson and Washington once more: "Peace, *commerce*, and honest friendship with all nations—entangling alliances with none"; and, "The Great rule of conduct for us, in regard to foreign Nations, is *in extending our commercial relations* to have with them as little political connection as possible." Washington in particular was quite clear on the value of an unimpeded commerce with the rest of the world: "Harmony, liberal intercourse with all Nations are recommended by policy, humanity, and interest. But even our Commercial policy should hold an equal and impartial hand; neither seeking nor receiving exclusive favors or preferences; consulting the natural course of things; diffusing and diversifying by gentle means the stream of Commerce but forcing nothing . . ."

In the Libertarian view, this means the elimination of government interference in international trade—the end of the Export-Import Bank, the International Monetary Fund, foreign aid, and the other methods used for decades now to manipulate the economies of other nations and tie them by artificial means to our own. It means the end to protective tariffs—which among other things not only stunt the growth of Third World countries, but lower the standard of living of American consumers. It means the termination of government credit guarantees to privileged exporters, and the cessation of U.S. interference in the internal affairs of other nations—via the CIA and other instruments—in order to protect foreign investments. And, in particular, it means an end to the use of foreign trade as a weapon, denying or curtailing it in response to various political moves by other nations of which we may disapprove. The senselessness of economic sanctions against Iran and the Soviet Union seems to be obvious to everyone but the policy makers in Washington. Utterly unenforceable, and never having succeeded in the past, economic sanctions only embitter relations with foreign countries, rally their peoples around the very policies of their governments they are intended to undermine, and cost American producers and consumers (and, in the case of the grain embargo against the Soviet Union, taxpayers also) dearly.

It is in this fashion—by forcing nothing and leaving international commerce to the free-flowing action of the market—that trade can become an agency for peace rather than for distrust, hostility, and war.

The reality is that what is setting the world in turmoil, for the most part, is not Soviet machinations, but nationalism. The nationalism of the countries of the Third World is understandable, given their colonial pasts. Unfortunately, many of these countries have surrendered to authoritarianism in politics and state-socialism in economics. This is truly tragic, since such totalitarianism, in the nature of things, can lead to nothing but aggravated misery for their peoples. But here, too, a policy of nonintervention by the United States can be beneficial. It will end the association in the minds of the educated elites between imperialism and capitalism, and direct their ire against whatever other foreign powers choose to continue meddling in their affairs. And it may eventually occur to the decision-makers and molders of public opinion in the Third World nations (as it has, for instance, to a few African leaders) that they have little to fear from foreign investors who are not backed by the military and diplomatic power of their home countries. American industry and finance have a great deal to offer the developing countries; removing their connection to the American government will enable them to do it.

Finally, Libertarians are not "isolationists" because we believe that the United States, as a nation, has a great role to play in the world still. But the role for us is not that of global policeman, or enforcer of some kind of global order, designed in advance and defended by Marines against the desires of others. Rather, it is to act as a model and a beacon to the peoples of the earth. As political scientist and foreign policy analyst Earl C. Ravenal has said: "Our primary business is to operate our unique political system, enjoy and enhance our economic activities, and repair and perfect our society.'' In this way, the United States can once again become the inspiration to those everywhere striving for liberty, and "America" a shorthand way of saying the Good Life, of freedom and abundance, for people the world over.

CHAPTER 5:

The Energy Crisis: Made in Washington

The matters I've discussed in the preceding chapters—the crushing burden of government, the devastating inflation, the incredible dangers of our irrational foreign policy—all come ominously together in the so-called energy crisis. Does anyone need further proof of the government's impotence in solving problems? The energy crisis should convince everyone of the government's ability to do one thing well, though: create problems.

Since 1973 American presidents have gone on television more times than any of us likes to recall, in order to persuade the American people of our grave energy crisis—usually to blame us for it—and to unveil yet another grand program. If only we weren't so selfish and stupid, they tell us, we could make energy more plentiful, reduce imports from OPEC, assure that poor people have access to gasoline and heating oil, and keep the oil companies from "profiteering" from our misfortune.

What is there to show for all this crisis-mongering? Energy prices continue to rise rapidly, supplies are uneven, and the risk of war to protect "American oil interests" in the Middle East grows. Besides this, we face daily threats to our personal liberty from proposed rationing plans and restrictions on auto use, new gasoline taxes, thermostat regulations, and government-sponsored synthetic-fuel production (funded by subsidies to Big Oil) that will claim massive amounts of scarce resources.

Moreover, the American people have been saddled with a new cabinet-level department, the Department of Energy, with a staff of more than 20,000 restless bureaucrats and a 1981 budget of at least $8.7 billion. This department, while it has thrown many obstacles in the way of energy producers, has yet to produce a single barrel of oil or cubic-foot of natural gas.

The contradictions in government policy give the energy situation an Alice-in-Wonderland atmosphere. It's a classic illustration of what happens when government tries to help us. Consider these:

● The government says we need to expand domestic production, but for nine years it has held the price of crude oil below the market level and has now passed a tax on the new revenues that will result from eventual decontrol (misnamed "windfall profits").

● The government says it is wrong for the oil companies to raise prices and profit from it; but then President Carter turns around and tries to hike the *tax* on gasoline by 10¢ a gallon, increasing revenues. (In other words, it is evil for producers to profit from expanding needed production, but okay for government officials who produce nothing to profit from other people's activities.)

● The government says Americans must conserve oil and gasoline, yet it has held the price artificially low for years with price controls, stimulating consumption.

● The government says we must cut foreign oil imports to maintain our independence, yet it impedes domestic production with taxes and regulations, and *subsidizes* imports with its entitlement program.

● The government has severely restricted the ability of oil companies to conduct their business, yet it has subsidized those same companies through its Mideast foreign policy and research-and-development grants. The synfuel program is only the latest subsidy for the large oil companies.

Given this hodge-podge of contradictions—this alternating obstruction and pampering of producers and consumers—is anyone surprised at the energy mess we confront today?

One question that public officials have never answered to the satisfaction of the American people is this: Is there really an energy crisis? Many people have a stake in making us think there is. Recipients of Energy Department subsidies obviously do. So do the 20,000 DOE employees, who would be out of jobs if it turned out the crisis didn't exist. So does the Carter

Administration, which has tried to use the crisis—the "moral equivalent of war"—to promote solidarity and patriotism, that is, to stifle criticism of the President's performance.

But *is* there really a crisis? Is the world running out of oil? Does OPEC have America over a barrel? Why have we suddenly become so aware of energy? Let's look at the facts.

The beginning of the energy crisis is set in 1973, when, during the Arab-Israeli war, the OPEC nations embargoed oil shipments to the United States. But two significant events that occurred two years earlier are somehow forgotten when this matter is discussed. In 1971, as part of President Nixon's Economic Stabilization Program, the U.S. government stopped redeeming dollars held by foreign governments for gold and froze all domestic prices. Price controls on crude oil and gasoline remain in effect to this day.

The first action prompted a great price rise by the OPEC nations, because their export dollars, depreciating every day just like yours and mine, were buying less and less. In other words, OPEC raised its prices not so much to get more real wealth from Americans, but to maintain the previous terms of trade. Americans are understandably upset by rising gasoline prices.

This rise has been caused by two things: the federal government's inflationary monetary policy, and the reduction in supply induced by price controls and restrictions on exploration of off-shore and government-held lands. The policy of the U.S. government, keeping price controls on domestic oil, and subsidizing importers, known as the "entitlements system," propelled the OPEC price even higher than it otherwise would have been.

While the price of oil has gone up as quoted in U.S. dollars, its price in terms of real commodities has risen far less. In terms of gold and silver, the price has even fallen. Back when gasoline was 25 cents a gallon, you could enter a gas station, give the attendant a quarter and he would give you a gallon of gasoline. That quarter was made of silver. Today, if you gave that *same* quarter to the attendant, he'd give you a gallon of gas and some change. (Silver quarters have been worth at least $2.50 recently.) The point is that the price of gas in silver has *dropped* over the past 20 years. If the problem is with the money, then, as we discussed in Chapter 3, the fault is with the government.

The second Nixon action—price controls—discouraged domestic producers from expanding their production of crude oil. Price controls always cause shortages and consumer lines because they over-stimulate consumption and discourage production. Lines don't occur when the price is free to rise and reflect new supply-and-demand conditions. While Americans were waiting in long lines in the spring of 1979, German and Japanese gasoline buyers were not, despite their greater use of OPEC oil. The reason: those nations had no price controls.

Government interference with the energy industry goes back further than 1971. Since the 1930s, Texas, with the blessing of the federal government and some of the oil companies, dictated production levels in the name of conservation, but actually as a way to keep the price up. Natural gas prices were controlled beginning in 1954. And in 1959, the U.S. government imposed quotas on cheap, competitive oil imports from the Middle East, in response to which OPEC was formed. As economist Edward J. Mitchell of the University of Michigan has written, "From the 1930s to at least 1970 . . . the U.S. crude oil producing market was not free. It was cartelized. . . . There was nothing unusual or devious about the domestic production cartel. It was established by state laws [and] endorsed by federal law."

Until the 1970s, government policy created a surplus of oil by keeping the price artificially high, and discouraging consumption. Since then, the policy has produced shortages by keeping the price low and stimulating consumption. Writes Mitchell, "The shortage of energy now facing the nation is not a problem for public policy—it *is* a public policy."

From the beginning of the "crisis" we have seen new controls imposed to try to correct the problems of previous controls. Invariably, things got worse. Nixon's Operation Independence, which included price and allocation controls, brought worse service for consumers and increased imports. The entitlements program adopted by President Ford's Federal Energy Administration did the same. (The program was supposed to equalize the average cost of crude oil between refiners who use artificially cheap domestic oil and those who use expensive imports. Thus it paid refiners to import.)

President Carter has acted in the meddling tradition of his predecessors. His multiple attempts at an energy program have involved extending controls on natural gas to intrastate markets, a wellhead tax on crude oil, and slow phasing out of price controls (encouraging producers to wait until the controls end in 1981). They also include a "windfall profits" tax that will divert $227 billion to the government over the next decade. This seems like a perverse way of coping with an "energy shortage." Who is more likely to use that money to produce energy, private industry or the government?

Meanwhile, the allocation program continues irrationally to distribute gasoline regardless of changes in consumer demand, and the Energy Department seeks to placate diverse special interests by constructing a crazy-quilt of regulations and exemptions. The chief casualty has been the freedom of producers and consumers to make their own decisions.

The point is that there *is* no energy crisis. What we have rather is a political crisis. The world is not running out of oil. Ever since the first well was drilled in Titusville, Pennsylvania, in 1859, people have been predicting that the last barrel was about to be produced. Yet much of the world has barely been explored for oil. As economics writer Jude Wanniski put it, "If you took all the liquid petroleum produced from all the wells on earth since the first . . . and poured it into a lake the size of Chicago, roughly 227 square miles, the 330 billion barrels the earth has yielded so far would fill the lake to a depth of only 300 feet. The estimated petroleum, worldwide, that could be recovered *at current prices and technology* would fill the lake to a depth of 2,300 feet." (Emphasis added.)

The energy crisis, then, is another hoax sponsored by the U.S. government. We, the consumers and taxpayers, have been made to pay the tremendous price—in discomfort and anxiety, in money, in lost liberty. It's time to call a halt to this travesty.

What is the Libertarian solution that I propose to the American people? It is simple and radical—the only one equal to the task. My proposal is to let the free market work. This means my administration will remove the obstacles that raise the cost to the industry of serving consumers in an orderly, efficient and just manner, and sometimes prohibit them from doing so altogether. What's more, my administration will move to eliminate all subsidies to energy firms. Oil companies and all other energy firms should have to make it on their own without shifting the risks to the taxpayers.

Specifically, I will seek to abolish the Department of Energy, which has no redeeming social value whatsoever. Rather, it is a millstone around the neck of the economy. I will seek to repeal all controls on prices, allocation and imports. I will act to repeal the entitlements program and the "windfall profits" tax, which has nothing to do with windfalls or profits. This tax does *not* apply to the oil producer's revenues in excess of costs. It applies rather to the difference between the controlled price of a barrel of oil and its market price, even if there is no profit. President Carter called for the tax on grounds that oil producers (10,000 of them produce 90 percent of the crude in the U.S.) haven't earned that increase. Think for a moment what an un-American principle that is. It is equivalent to saying that if the price of your home rises because market conditions change, you don't have a right to the profit when you sell because you didn't earn it. Who has a right to it? The government, says Carter.

Does that make sense to you? Is that how the system of free trade and property rights is supposed to work? As I understand that system, the mere act of buying a value at a lower price and selling it at a higher price is to earn the *profit* that results. We have let the politicians turn the principle of equity on its head long enough.

There is another important point to consider with regard to the "windfall profits tax" and our energy problem in general. Government propaganda has tried to make these issues into a little morality play, with the big bad oil companies on one side, and the virtuous Washington bureaucrats on the other. To a large extent, this attempt has succeeded—which suggests that the government is better at manipulating minds than at anything else. But the dichotomy is a false one. What we really have in the energy field is a government penalizing some, but *favoring* and *subsidizing* others. Consider the following news item, from the *Wall Street Journal* (Feb. 25, 1980):

> The creation of a $20 billion government synthetic fuels program may in turn be creating another institution: the energy-industrial complex. The terms of the alliance are being set this month, as House-Senate conferees complete work on legislation that seeks to combat the energy crisis by offering federal support for development of synthetic fuels. Corporate lobbyists, meanwhile, have been working overtime to make sure the program includes specific provisions that would benefit their companies. "It's a symbiotic relationship, like what you see between defense contractors and the Pentagon," says one oil-company lobbyist who has been watching the legislative dance.

The facade of government involvement in energy is that of a holy crusade against mean, old oil profiteers. The reality is a behind-the-scenes, dog-eat-dog struggle by various energy producers—sure to expand, as the stakes get larger and larger—for privileges and subsidies. Thus politics replaces the market, and the criterion for success is not whether you can cut costs and produce most efficiently, but whether you have political pull. The relatively clean world of supply and demand gives way to the world of the John Connallys and the Billy Carters.

We have already seen some of the effects of government favoritism in the case of nuclear power. Nuclear power is a creature of government from head to toe. It was developed by government, pushed on an unwilling private economy by government and subsidized and regulated by government at every stage. Perhaps the most dangerous subsidy has been the Price-Anderson Act, which has forced the taxpayers to bear much of the risk for nuclear accidents and arbitrarily limits the amount of money a plant is liable for in the event of an accident to $560 million. Not only don't the utilities have to pay the full cost of their insurance, but if they have an accident, they are not obligated to reimburse their victims more than a total of $560 million.

What we have ended up with is a nuclear-power industry inherently less safe than the free market would have produced, had it produced one at all. It stands to reason that if someone is not to be held fully responsible for his actions, he will have less incentive to be careful.

As President I will work to abolish the Price-Anderson Act and all subsidies to and regulations on the nuclear power industry. I will remove the government from the nuclear fuel cycle, and utilities will be liable for any damage to life and property resulting from the conduct of their business and the disposal of spent fuel. One of two things will happen: Either a safe industry will emerge in the free market, or, if that is impossible, no industry will emerge. Either way, we will be safer than we are today. The bureaucrats in government just cannot be trusted with such an important matter.

Desubsidizing nuclear power, incidentally, is in everyone's interest, including the power companies, if their product is indeed as safe as they claim. Their clinging to government protection, especially in insurance, gives credence to their critics. If they are truly confident about the safety of nuclear power, they have no reason to object to the repeal of Price-Anderson.

By the same token, I will seek to remove the subsidies and regulations from all energy forms. No one can say for certain what kinds of energy will emerge as the best. Solar, wind, gasohol, biomass—all may play a role in the future. Only the market will tell. But that means that each must be left to stand the test of the free market without subsidy or regulation. We must not make the mistake of centralizing alternative energy sources through government intervention, which distorts the natural direction of their growth. I don't want to see solar power follow the same route as nuclear power; the last thing we need is a "Solar Regulatory Commission" to copy the mistakes of the Nuclear Regulatory Commission. Only in a free market will we know what forms of energy are most economical.

In short, my solution to the energy crisis is to allow prices to reflect the realities of supply and demand. This is the only way to safeguard the liberty, prosperity, and security of the American people. Energy, obviously, is critical to our standard of living. Its management is too important to be left to the same people who run Amtrak and the Post Office. The libertarian solution relies instead on the decentralized management of the free-market economy, in which firms compete to satisfy consenting consumers. Surely that is preferable to relying on the bureaucratic DOE, which, because it gets its funds from captive taxpayers, need satisfy no one, expect perhaps a President seeking reelection.

My proposal, you'll notice, calls for *immediate* freeing of the market. In the name of liberty and prosperity, *we must not merely phase out* the controls. Prolonging the controls only prolongs the hardship. When Washington imposed price controls during both world wars, shortages quickly developed. When the controls were removed after the wars, the nation soon had plentiful supplies at low prices. The same thing will happen when we free the energy market today. New opportunities for profit will stimulate production and innovation, insuring adequate quantities of energy products at the lowest possible cost.

I would like to close this chapter by addressing the most dangerous aspect of this problem. American foreign policy is becoming fatefully entwined with energy policy. One reason the U.S. government wishes to cut oil imports and end our energy-dependency is to maintain its "flexibility" in foreign policy. "Flexibility" means the ability to intervene in the affairs of other nations whenever our leaders are moved to do so; the dangers of such a foreign policy stance were presented in Chapter Four.

Our government should neither restrict imports *nor* attempt to protect oil interests in the Middle East. Americans should be free to buy any imports; if imported products are less expensive, it makes sense to buy them and thus maximize our assets. At the same time, the domestic industry should be free to produce so that there are alternatives to uncertain foreign supplies. But we should reject the prejudice against imports and the fear of so-called interdependence. Free trade is the greatest guarantor of peace. Communities that are benefitting from trade with each other are a lot less likely to fight.

As for OPEC, it is another creature of U.S. policy. We have seen that OPEC's "aggressive" policies were direct responses to American monetary actions. Its power, likewise, is merely the result of the crippling of the domestic industry by controls and subsidies. OPEC, in fact, does not behave like a classic cartel. Most OPEC nations do not restrict supply; only Saudi Arabia and Kuwait deliberately hold back to influence price. But they would lose that ability if the U.S. industry were unleashed.

In reality, there is an *implicit* cartel operating. It consists of OPEC and the DOE (which has restrained OPEC's competition: domestic producers). I am all for eliminating that cartel by abolishing the Department of Energy.

I cannot stress enough the importance of breaking the connection between foreign policy and energy policy. This has been one of the most dangerous follies our government has indulged itself in. For example, there is substantial evidence that the former Shah of Iran was supported in his efforts to dramatically boost OPEC prices from 1973 to 1977 by then Secretary of State Henry Kissinger, who wanted the shah to have the means to buy massive amounts of American armaments. Freeing the domestic industry would have lowered the price of petroleum, but that would have clashed with the Nixon-Kissinger foreign-policy objective of making the shah a powerful client.

We cannot afford to continue the approach of alternately subsidizing and hobbling energy. By ending the political crisis, we will deprive the politicians of their favorite pretext for raising taxes, multiplying restrictions on our liberty, meddling abroad, registering our youth for a military draft, and generally preparing for war. I'd say it's well worth it.

CHAPTER 6:

Education in America: The Need for Choice

The quality of education in America has been steadily declining for the past fifteen years. Yet the politicians don't talk much about education. Why? I suspect that they're afraid to discuss the subject because they haven't the slightest idea of what to do about it. I think education should be a major issue in this election, and I intend to make it one. The future of the next generation is at stake.

How do we know the quality of education is declining? The evidence is clear and convincing. For the past sixteen years, average scores on the Scholastic Aptitude Test (SAT) have steadily fallen. In math, they've gone from 502 in 1963 to 467 in 1978. The decline is even worse in verbal scores—from 474 to 427 in the same period of time. Since the base score on each test is 200, that actually amounts to a 14 percent overall drop, or almost 1 percent a year.

At the Berkeley campus of the University of California, where entering freshmen come from the top one-eighth of high school graduates, nearly half the freshmen in a recent entering class needed remedial English courses. Employers find high school and even college graduates unable to spell and punctuate, much less compose readable reports.

It's no wonder, of course, that our children don't learn much in the government schools, considering the conditions there. Especially—though not exclusively—in urban areas, schools have become physically dangerous places. The National Association of School Security Directors has reported that in 1976 there were 8,000 rapes, 11,000 armed robberies, 256,000 burglaries and 190,000 major assaults in the schools. The National Institute of Education reported in 1978 that in a given month some 2.4 million secondary school students have something stolen from them and 282,000 are attacked. Many schools now

60

have bars on the windows and policemen patrolling the halls, hardly a good environment for learning. The Carnegie Council on Policy Studies in Higher Education wrote recently, "High school is an alienating experience for many young people [and] like a prison—albeit with open doors—for some."

At the same time that real education is declining, costs are soaring. The cost of government education per pupil has risen from about $920 to over $1500 in the past twenty years—and that figure is adjusted for inflation. Just in the last decade per-pupil costs have climbed 155 percent while the consumer price index rose only 69 percent. Are we hiring fewer teachers for our children? No—the ratio of students to teachers was 25-1 in 1960, and it had fallen to 18-1 by 1975. The number of administrative personnel has risen even faster. In 1950 there was one full-time educational employee for each 19 students. By 1978 the figure was one for each nine students.

With all this increased spending, why has the quality of education fallen? Perhaps the first lesson to be learned is that increased spending does not necessarily improve education. Indeed, experts have said recently that there is *no* evidence that increased spending has any positive impact on educational achievement at all. The experience of the last two decades—soaring costs and falling test scores—would certainly lead one to such a conclusion.

A more basic problem is the nature of government education. Compulsory attendance laws and monopoly schools force the same kind of education on students with widely varying abilities and interests. Many young people would prefer to be working, reading in a library, traveling, or engaging in any number of activities other than school. Why should the government force them to attend school when they would prefer to be learning from life?

For years, educators, parents, and government officials have been wrangling over what constitutes a good education. Our school districts are constant battlegrounds between conflicting forces. There are those who want to go back to basics—the three R's—while others prefer an unstructured curriculum. Some want prayer in schools; others want sex education. Some want to exclude gay teachers; others want a positive discussion

61

of "alternative lifestyles." Some want to teach evolution, others the Biblical story of creation. Some want special treatment for gifted children, others don't.

As economist Walter Williams, who grew up in the Philadelphia ghetto and now teaches at Temple University, wrote recently,

> A state monopoly in the production of a good or service enhances the potential for conflict, through requiring uniformity; that is, its production requires a *collective* decision on many attributes of the product, and once produced, everybody has to consume the identical product whether he agrees with all the attributes or not. State monopolies in the production of education enhance the potential for conflict by requiring conformity on issues of importance to many people. For example, prayers in school, ethnic history, saluting the flag and educational tracking are highly controversial issues which have received considerable court attention and have resulted in street fighting and heightened racial tensions.

With all this conflict raging, what is the result? Some groups "win," and the schools reflect their values. But others are then forced to send their children to schools of which they don't approve. These conflicts are unavoidable in any government controlled system. As long as the schools are supported by taxes, different groups of taxpayers will compete to control them.

The public schools are a classic example of the problems of bureaucracy. The schools are not run by parents or teachers but by professional administrators. The administrators are not paid on the basis of their performance, and they have no incentive to improve the educational achievements of their students. The number of people employed in the education bureaucracy has risen faster than the number of teachers in recent years, and far faster than the number of students. This means more expense, more paperwork, and more obstacles to any real learning.

There are many dedicated teachers in the public school system, but for the most part they are victims of the system. They must deal with a sluggish, top-heavy bureaucracy, with "approved" textbooks, with government prescriptions on the "right" way to teach, and with a host of petty rules and regulations. They know that they will be rewarded not for merit, but for endurance. Indeed, creativity in the classroom may just run them afoul of some bureaucratic rule. Is it any wonder that they become resigned and disinterested?

One of my national campaign staffers used to teach in a public elementary school. When I asked her why she quit, she told me that she had tired of the "assembly-line" approach to education and the apparently uncontrollable violence Teachers found themselves spending much of their time drawing up proposals for federal grants and then filling out reports on the federally supported programs. Once, she said, a federal administrator came to her classroom to ask why she hadn't completed the paperwork on one program. "I can teach," she told him, "or I can fill out forms." Experiences like this led her to leave the public school system.

Unfortunately, this is the way bureaucracy works. It is not realistic to propose reform of the government school system; as long as schools are run by the government, they will be bureaucratic institutions, not centers of learning.

In the face of the sorry record of our public schools, what have my opponents proposed on the issue of education? For the most part, they have been silent—understandably so, given their records and their apparent inability to come to grips with the current crisis.

President Carter has increased federal spending on education by about 60 percent in two and a half years. Aside from the increased burden on already hard-pressed taxpayers that this represents, it should be clear by now that increased spending on education does *not* lead to improved results. And, of course, President Carter established the Department of Education. I'll have more to say about that in a minute, but for now let me just say that centralization of our educational system in Washington is not what we need. No improvement in our educational system has taken place under the Carter administration, and he has given us no reason to expect any.

Ronald Reagan says he opposes the Department of Education and the centralization of educational decision-making away from the local level. But let's look at his record. Reagan increased spending on the state colleges by 163 percent during his two terms as Governor of California. Spending on the state university system more than doubled. Reagan created the California Maritime Academy and the California Space Institute, two new boondoggles for the taxpayers to support. And Governor Reagan contributed substantially to the transfer of power from the local school district to the state government. He created a new statewide Board of Governors to oversee the community college system, as well as a state Commission on Educational Reform. And he dramatically increased the percentage of educational funds coming from the state government rather than in local revenues. As the San Francisco *Chronicle* wrote recently, though Reagan's campaign for President is stressing the theme of returning government to the local level, his record as Governor of California was exactly the opposite.

John Anderson's record on education is clear. During his twenty years in Congress he has consistently supported increased federal spending on education and centralization of educational decision making. He has supported mandatory busing and other measures to increase federal control over our educational system. He was a long-time backer of a federal Department of Education. On the issue of education, there's no "Anderson difference" from the failed policies of the past.

Fortunately, many parents seem to understand the basic problem with government schools better than the politicians do. Parents are increasingly turning to alternatives to the government schools. In the last decade, while public school enrollments actually fell about 4 percent, the number of students in non-sectarian private schools increased about 60 percent. And the parents who are choosing alternative schools are not always wealthy; in fact, 38 percent of the children in non-government schools come from families with annual incomes below $15,000.

One of the encouraging things about the increase in educational alternatives is their diversity. Many parents, of course, send their children to traditional elite private schools or to

Catholic parochial schools. But many new "Christian schools" affiliated with conservative Protestant denominations are springing up, especially in the South. And contrary to some media reports, these schools are not racially motivated or all-white. Black enrollment in the three largest Christian schools in the Washington, D.C. suburbs is estimated at 10 to 20 percent. In another alternative to public schools, more and more Jewish parents are sending their children to Hebrew Day Schools.

In New York thousands of black parents, disgusted with the poor performance of inner-city government schools, are sending their children to black-run private schools. These schools stress self-discipline, parent involvement, and educational achievement. One black parent quoted in the *New York Times* said of her decision to place her son in a private school in Harlem, "The public schools couldn't develop my son's potential, and they were well on the way to damaging him as a student. [Private school] is an expense I can hardly afford, but a parent has to make these sacrifices. You simply cannot place your child's future in the hands of officials in the public school system."

In Chicago, there's a waiting list of 850 students—all black—at Westside Prep, a one-room school run by the remarkable Marva Collins. Mrs. Collins takes students who have been declared "retarded," "brain-damaged," "slow," or "troublesome" by the public schools—and she teaches them. Her 6 to 12-year-old students, judged failures in the public schools, read Thoreau, Shakespeare, and Sophocles, write essays, and learn mathematics. Marva Collins refuses government aid in order to keep her independence, and she doesn't use any teaching machines or audio-visual equipment, believing that all education requires is a teacher and a student.

Across the country, in Los Angeles, parents fed up with the public schools decided to build their own. They pooled their funds, bought land, built the schools, hired the teachers, and planned the curriculum. As columnist Richard Reeves wrote in *Esquire*, "They simply took over—or took back—a function of a government they detested. In the words I heard over and over again from angry, exhilirated parents: 'We took control of our own lives!' "

In an even more individualistic spirit, more and more parents are teaching their children at home. Despite great legal harassment from state authorities, they believe they can give their children a better education at home than in any school. Thomas Hempel, the president of the Port Byron, New York, school board says, "I really think the public school system turns out mental and moral cripples." So he teaches three of his children at home. Parents in many states have faced legal challenges to their decision to educate their children at home. And in a particularly tragic case of the government's desperate battle to preserve its monopoly, Mormon fundamentalist John Singer was shot in the back and killed when ten Utah police officers came to his mountain farm to seize his children and take them to public school. Fortunately, most legal battles have ended more peacefully, and some courts are even recognizing the right of parents to educate their own children as they choose.

I think the vitality and diversity of these educational alternatives is encouraging. Different parents want different kinds of educational experiences for their children, and such schools reflect this; but they are all agreed that their children need a good education, and that they don't get it in the public schools.

Why do non-government schools seem to do a much better job than government schools? There are several reasons. They are not afflicted with the bureaucracy of the public schools. To keep their expenses down, they have to eliminate waste and excessive overhead. Without a bottomless pit of tax money available to them, they can't afford to hire useless administrative personnel. Instead of following a set of rules and regulations drawn up in district headquarters, or the state capital, or Washington, they concentrate on *teaching* and *learning*

And parents, who have to pay directly for their children's education, have an incentive to pay attention to their achievement. If a private school fails to educate, it learns about the problem in a very direct way: its students go elsewhere. This emphasis on learning, not bureaucracy, encourages teachers to perform better.

And instead of the political conflict over what is taught in

66

the public schools, independent schools have only one group to satisfy: students and their parents. They offer a particular kind of education, and if some parents don't like it, they choose another school. It would be very hard to find anyone at a private school who would say what Albert Shanker, President of the American Federation of Teachers, said to the *New York Times* (Dec. 30, 1979): "The purpose of education is not particularly to make one parent or another happy. There are certain social and public purposes to public education." "Purposes"defined, of course, not by parents or students, but by educational bureaucrats like Shanker.

What lies behind all these differences between government and non-government schools? It is the issue of coercion, or force. The public schools, paid for with taxes, corraling students with compulsory attendance laws, operating under a strict set of regulations, are based on coercion. But education is a personal, dynamic process that doesn't work well in an atmosphere of force. A private school, based on voluntary choice and voluntary funding, is a much better place for learning to occur.

This being the case, why, then, haven't more parents turned to nongovernment education? I think there is one basic answer: cost. Parents are already paying exorbitant tax burdens for the government schools. Paying again for a private school may be impossible, when tuition can run from $500 up to $7,000 per year, with the average about $1,100. It's a tribute to the overwhelming desire of parents to educate their children that so many do make this sacrifice.

But what about the parents who can't afford to bear the extra cost of tuition on top of their school taxes? What about the people who have no choice but to accept the fact that their children may never get a decent education? Our present system means that most of those who are now poor and uneducated are condemned to remain poor and uneducated because they are denied the opportunity to break out of this vicious cycle, to get a good education and a good start on life. And even middle-class parents are condemned to send their children to inferior schools.

There is a basic fallacy cherished by the education bureaucracy that is undermining the quality of education in this country and may ensure that disadvantaged children will remain disadvantaged and dependent on the rest of society.

That fallacy is that there is only one "right" way to educate a child, that children aren't individual human beings with their own needs, talents, and interests, and that parents and children should accept whatever educational theory the monopoly system of public education is promoting at the moment.

If the education bureaucrats decide to teach the three R's, or sex education, or the Biblical account of creation, that's what they'll teach. And whatever their decision is, at least some parents, teachers, and children will remain unhappy and unfulfilled. For what is missing in our educational system today is *freedom to choose*—the right to determine what kind of education is best for our own children.

These are *our* children, and children and parents are individual human beings who should have the absolute right to make the fundamental decisions about their future, such as what kind of education they will have. Government has taken this right away from us, and the result has been disastrous.

If we are to restore the hope of quality education for all, we must guarantee our right to choose.

In 1978, as a candidate for Governor of California, I proposed a new alternative for our educational system. My proposal was widely discussed, and has been incorporated into an initiative sponsored by the National Taxpayers Union which will eventually be voted on by the people of California.

What I proposed was a system of education tax credits to enable parents—not the government—to choose the education they want for their children.

As a candidate for President, I'm continuing to make education and my tax credit proposal a leading feature of my campaign. My proposal would grant a tax credit of up to $1200 off the top for the education of each child from each eligible individual's federal income tax. The credit would apply to elementary, secondary, or college education at either government or nongovernment schools.

Under such a program, parents and children will be able to afford to choose the education they think best.

Such tax credits allow freedom to choose among educational alternatives to middle and upper income people. But what about lower-income people, whose taxes are too low to take advantage of a full tax credit?

I would extend the opportunity to take an education tax credit to *anyone* who pays for the education of a child. Relatives or friends of the children involved, as well as any other concerned taxpayers, will be eligible for the credit.

Even corporations would receive this tax credit if they paid for the education of children who would not otherwise benefit from the tax credit. They could take such credits (at up to $1200 per student) up to 25 percent of their total federal tax liability.

By opening up the availability of the tax credit to everyone, we'll create a tremendous incentive for people to take a personal interest in providing quality education, particularly to lower income children, the ones who suffer most from our present educational system.

That's why black leaders like Roy Innis, national director of the Congress on Racial Equality, are supporting a tax-credit program. Innis wrote recently, "This will have a revolutionary effect on millions of poor parents and children in this country. Those are the parents and children who until now have had no choice—and with no choice, no power . . . We are proposing that we shift the power from those who control (i.e., the educational establishment) to those they control (parents and kids)."

And one of the nation's most distinguished black economists, Professor Thomas Sowell of UCLA, has written, a tuition tax credit

is most important to those who are mentioned least: the poor, the working class, and all whose children are trapped in educationally deteriorating and physically dangerous public schools. Few groups have so much at stake in the fate of this (program) as ghetto blacks . . .

The crux of the controversy is *choice* and *power*. If parents are given a choice, public school officials will lose the monopoly power they now hold over a captive audience. That monopoly power is greatest over the poor, but it extends to all who cannot afford to simultaneously pay taxes for the public schools and tuition at a private school.

I think our society will be much better educated and more harmonious when such fundamental responsibilities as education are discharged by the individuals who are most concerned—parents and students.

What does my tax credit proposal do to public education? At the very least, it will introduce an element of fair competition into education which can only be beneficial. In business, what usually happens when one company has a monopoly? It becomes fat and lazy and fails to respond to the changing demands of its customer, until a competitor springs up to challenge it. I would expect that this system of tax credits might even improve public education by providing some healthy competition. And if public education does not improve, then, like any other good or service in the marketplace, it will attract a smaller and smaller share of the market while its more creative, innovative, and responsive competitors continue to upgrade their product.

On the issue of education, the first priority of a Libertarian administration would be to establish this system of education tax credits which would open up free choice in education to all.

A Libertarian administration would have another task to deal with as well. That is to reverse the trend toward centralizing control of education in Washington.

Not too long ago, President Carter—the same president who said he would streamline the federal government—created a brand-new Cabinet Department, the Department of Education. To me, this is like trying to put out a fire with gasoline. Government control of education has failed, and you don't solve the problem by creating another multi-billion-dollar layer of bureaucracy. Carter supported creation of the department to pay off a campaign debt to the National Education Association. "We're the only union with our own Cabinet department," one NEA official boasted when the new department was established. But I think the Department of Education is a big mistake. As the New York *Times* editorialized, "The supporters of a separate department speak vaguely of the need for a Federal policy on education. We believe that they misunderstand the nature of American education, which is characterized by diversity." The Department of Education is another expensive intrusion into our freedom to choose, and I would abolish it.

But ultimately, I believe, a Libertarian administration must go further than these two reforms. Let me be clear on this point: It is fundamentally contrary to the principles of a free society for government to involve itself in education. I believe as strongly in the separation of education and state as I do in the separation of church and state, and for the very same reasons.

I think we would all look with horror on a society in which the government published 90 percent of the books available in America. I think it is just as dangerous for 90 percent of our children to be educated in government schools. The dangers inherent in such a near-monopoly go well beyond the decline in educational quality. We all know what happens when a totalitarian regime seizes power in another country: One of the first things it does is to restructure the educational system to fit its way of thinking. Even taking a much more benign view of our own government, how can a government school system help but to promote the basic values of the people in power? The public-school interpretation of American history, politics, and economics must necessarily coincide with what the government thinks is correct. It's certainly worth noting that economics as taught in the public schools is almost exclusively of the Keynesian variety—the economic doctrine that has justified massive government intervention in the economy, the boom-and-bust cycle of inflation and recession, and now the phenomenon known as "stagflation."

Americans traditionally have valued freedom of speech highly enough to keep government from legislating against it. We have valued freedom of religion enough to prohibit government from interfering in its free exercise and from establishing a state religion. These traditions recognize the dangers of letting government involve itself in the world of ideas. It is time that we establish freedom of education, which, after all, intimately involves both speech and religion, and remove government from this area altogether.

Let me conclude this chapter by describing my vision of education in America. A child's education is and should be an intensely personal and private matter. The principal decisions should be made by parents and children—for it is their lives that are affected. I want to reduce the role of impersonal, unresponsive government in this decision, and instead enhance the role of free individuals. I want to invite all members of society, whether they are parents or not, to take an active interest in and responsibility for education, by breaking away from the notion that government, after all these years, can be expected to find a solution for our educational problems. I want to have an environment in which all children have the opportunity to reach their highest potential, whatever that may be, in freedom—without being forced into a mold by a government bureaucracy. I envision a system which encourages a young and curious mind to know the joy of learning, not one which stifles this process and turns joy into a burden.

I want to see people in voluntary interaction build an educational system that will be a reflection of a creative, dynamic, peaceful, and voluntary society. We can start by implementing a program of education tax credits and moving toward a free educational system.

CHAPTER 7:

Social Security: The Ultimate Pyramid Scheme

While I was thinking about this chapter, one of my campaign workers told me a story that couldn't have been more appropriate. He had recently been to a family dinner in Kentucky, and during a discussion of current events, someone mentioned Social Security. A young woman listening to the conversation, a hairdresser, sighed with resignation and said softly, ''There won't be any money there when we're ready to retire.'' Others agreed, echoing her despair.

Little did they suspect that a few days later, in June of 1980, *The Washington Post* would report:

> The enormous Social Security tax increases voted in 1977 will not be enough to keep the system solvent unless the nation's economy improves substantially, the system's trustees reported yesterday. William J. Driver, commissioner of Social Security, told reporters that *even under the most optimistic economic assumptions*, Social Security faces severe new short-run financial strains because of the national economic problems over the past few years, and *will not have enough money to pay old-age retirement benefits starting in 1982* unless Congress acts. (Emphasis added.)

And this even taking into account the massive increases in the payroll tax that will start next year! No doubt after reading that article, many more Americans share the woman's attitude about how well the federal government is planning for their retirement. After taking a healthy portion of their pay each week, ostensibly for old-age, disability, survivor and health insurance, the government now tells them there may be nothing left when they need their money. Of all of government's impositions on the lives and liberty of the American people, this has to be the cruelest.

The root of the Social Security problem is the same one that has been discussed throughout this book: the lack of liberty. You have no choice but to participate in Social Security, regardless of your means, values, tastes or preferences. (Federal employees are exempt. Do they know something we don't?) You may not decide for yourself how much you want to pay for insurance or how much you want to collect when you retire. Distant bureaucrats decide for you. You may not express your dissatisfaction with the system's administrators by cancelling your policy and finding another company. The administrators collect their salaries regardless of consumer satisfaction The public till doesn't require happy customers, just the power of taxation.

The Social Security system did not begin as an attempt to sabotage people's ability to plan for retirement, but it has worked out that way. The politicians who originally planned the system probably had no idea how it would turn out. But today's politicians know the system is rotted, and yet they refuse to make the changes necessary to free the American people from it. Instead, they make it worse. They promise benefits they know they may not be able to pay and enact tax increases that harm workers and the economy. In 1977 the politicians passed the largest peacetime tax increases in U.S. history to try to save Social Security. In 1950 the tax was 1.5 percent. Today it is 6.13 percent. Beginning January 1, 1981, it will be 6.65 percent. The maximum tax, which was $45 a year in 1950, will go from today's $1,587 to $1,975 in 1981.

And the government doesn't know if it'll be able to pay retirement benefits in 1982! Something is dreadfully wrong.

The Social Security system was started in 1935, during the Great Depression, ostensibly because many people's savings were wiped out by the economic debacle. For our purposes, it is important to realize that Social Security was started and continues to be maintained for two distinct purposes: insurance and welfare. It is considered insurance because payroll contributions entitle workers or their families to retirement, disability, survivor or health-care benefits when needed. It is considered welfare because the first recipients of benefits had paid nothing into the system and because benefits today are unrelated to how much a worker personally contributed.

The major source of trouble for the system, a consequence of the contradiction in purpose, is its pay-as-you-go method of funding. To understand how this works, imagine the following scheme: Someone offers to sell you an insurance policy. Weekly payments entitle you to benefits when you retire. Each week, when you send your money to the company, it turns around and pays out that money as benefits to others who were sold the same policy some time ago. The company plans to pay you retirement benefits from the payments made by people who'll be working after *you* retire.

If you think this sounds like one of those fraudulent pyramid schemes you read about in the papers occasionally, you are right. Would you choose to participate in such a plan if you knew the facts?

You are participating in one right now.

What was the original intention of Social Security? Many people thought it was supposed to be a pension fund, which would take each individual's contribution and invest it, returning that money, plus interest, to him on retirement. That's what the people were led to believe. Recently, however, a leading government bureaucrat was kind enough to disabuse them (San Francisco *Chronicle*, Nov. 30, 1979):

> Social Security Commissioner Sanford G. Ross said yesterday people must forget "myths" about contributing to their own retirement and recognize the payroll deduction for what it is—a tax to support the elderly, dis-, abled and their families. The myth that the Social Security levy was a contribution, not a tax, "proved valuable in the early days of the program, but . . . is helping to confuse the debate over Social Security today," he said.

In any case, the system today has a $4 *trillion* unfunded liability. If you are working today, your benefits will depend on the power of the government to tax those who will be working when you retire. The government hasn't husbanded your money. It has paid it out to current recipients whose own contributions were paid out to others long before they retired.

You can begin to appreciate why the system is so unstable, why bankruptcy chronically looms. It is completely at the mercy of changes in economic conditions and population trends. Inflation sends benefits climbing, but the accompanying unemployment diminishes wage-tax collections. The baby-boom/baby-bust cycle of the past 35 years will eventually mean a large retired population living off a relatively small working population. What guarantee do you have that Social Security will deliver on its promises? None.

By now, you are aware of a major difference between Social Security and private insurance plans. All private plans invest the premiums of their policyholders so that when the policy pays off, it returns both the original investment and interest. The terms are known in advance. Fraud can be redressed in the courts.

Not so with Social Security. Payment terms are not clearly spelled out. The system leads workers to believe that their employers pay half the tax. But this is not so. The *entire* tax actually comes from the employee, the "employer's share" being a labor cost that reduces what employers can pay directly to their workers.

Besides this, the Social Security tax increases passed by Congress are unrelated to the benefit structure. There is no certainty that Congress won't *cut* benefits when you retire, regardless of what you paid in during your working years.

A private company conducting business this way would be charged with fraud. But at the Social Security Administration, it is business as usual.

Social Security compares unfavorably with conventional private plans on many other counts. For example, in the private sphere, people can choose the plan best suited to their needs. Social Security has only one plan. Given the diversity of tastes and lifestyles in America, no single plan could possibly suit everyone. With a private plan, benefits are paid without strings; policyholders can collect a lump sum to invest or arrange to have it paid in increments. Social Security benefits are laden with restrictions. Benefits are paid monthly. Retired persons are limited in how much outside income they can make without losing benefits. Widows lose survivor benefits if they remarry. Etc., etc., etc.

The differences between Social Security and private insurance reach to the most fundamental level. With private insurance, consumers ultimately determine what services are offered. If they don't like one company's services, they are free to take their money to another. This is the most effective influence a consumer can have. It is absent in Social Security. Participants have no choice. They can't withdraw. They must take what they are given. Politicians and bureaucrats, whose incomes don't depend on the *consent* of the taxpayers, run the system. At best, if someone wants to change Social Security, he must organize a national movement to persuade Congress or elect a new Congress. Compare this nearly impossible task to the ease of cancelling a private policy you don't like and buying another one.

The principle involved is the one that distinguishes government from the free market. The administrators of Social Security have no incentive to satisfy their "customers." They can't be put out of business if people don't like their performance. They are immune from market forces. The results are predictable: A uniform, expensive system on the brink of bankruptcy. In contrast, the operators of private plans have no guarantees. They can't force anyone to patronize them. Again, the results are predictable: A wide range of services and prices reflecting the demands of consumers.

The difference this principle makes can be seen on the bottom line. Economists have estimated that the real rate of return on Social Security, after inflation, is 1-to-2 percent. Harvard economist Martin Feldstein estimates that with private insurance workers could look forward to a return of 13-to-15 percent.

This would have an enormous impact on our ability to plan for retirement. Social Security expert Peter Ferrara, reports that even for a low-wage earner, Social Security finishes a distant second. A young worker making $5,731 in 1980, if married, will receive annual Social Security benefits of $9,212 on retirement—92 percent of his last pre-retirement income. If he puts his Social Security payments into a private plan paying 6 percent, he will accumulate a trust fund of $299,450, which would pay annual interest of $17,967 when he retired—178 percent of his last pre-retirement income. Or he could buy an annuity that would pay him $33,894 for life. If his wife works, they could accumulate a fund of more than half a million dollars. If low-wage earners could leave that kind of legacy to their heirs, think of what would happen to the poverty cycle in this country.

The situation is analogous for a 24-year-old man beginning work in 1980 at $25,900 a year. He will be paid $12,125 a year in Social Security benefits on retirement, $18,188 if married. For the same money he paid in Social Security taxes, a private plan paying a real return of only 6 percent would accumulate a trust fund of $1,019,014! He could then live off the interest or buy a perpetual annuity paying $61,141 a year for life—132 percent of his last pre-retirement salary! When he dies, there'd be a million-dollar fund to leave to his heirs.

To appreciate how bad a "buy" Social Security is, remember that after these retired persons collect their interest or annuity payments from a private firm, they will still have a large trust fund to leave their children. In contrast, since Social Security benefits are unrelated to payments and the operation is pay-as-you-go, there is no trust fund. The benefits end when the retired person dies.

The Social Security system hurts specific groups in special ways, besides those already described. The poor are hurt because the payroll tax is regressive; in effect, they pay a greater percentage of their income than wealthier people because income over $25,000 is not taxed. They are worse off than wealthier people because they tend to start work earlier in life and die sooner. They are harmed worst of all because of Social Security's detrimental effects on the economy, which I'll discuss shortly.

The system discriminates against married working women, childless couples, and single people because Social Security was constructed with the traditional family in mind. A married, working woman who accepts spouse benefits on her husband's

Help Ed Clark's Libertarian Campaign... It's Time for A New Beginning

YES! I want to help distribute A New Beginning to my friends and neighbors. Please rush me the following number of books at quantity discount prices:

- [ ] 5 copies ($4.00)
- [ ] 100 copies ($40.00)
- [ ] 10 copies ($7.00)
- [ ] 500 copies ($150.00)
- [ ] 50 copies ($25.00)
- [ ] 1000 copies ($250.00)

(Add 20% for air express.)

Here's my contribution to the Clark campaign:

- [ ] $1000
- [ ] $500
- [ ] $100
- [ ] $50
- [ ] $25

Make checks payable to Clark for President.

Name _____

Address _____

City _____ State _____ Zip ____

Occupation _____

Business Address _____

NO POSTAGE
NECESSARY
IF MAILED
IN THE
UNITED STATES

BUSINESS REPLY MAIL

FIRST CLASS   PERMIT NO. 12388   WASHINGTON, DC

POSTAGE WILL BE PAID BY ADDRESSEE

CLARK
PRESIDENT
2300 Wisconsin Avenue, NW
Washington, DC 20007

Help Ed Clark's Libertarian Campaign . . . It's Time for A New Beginning

YES! I want to help distribute A New Beginning to my friends and neighbors. Please rush me the following number of books at quantity discount prices:

- ☐ 5 copies ($4.00)
- ☐ 10 copies ($7.00)
- ☐ 50 copies ($25.00)
- ☐ 100 copies ($40.00)
- ☐ 500 copies ($150.00)
- ☐ 1000 copies ($250.00)

(Add 20% for air express.)

Here's my contribution to the Clark campaign:

☐ $1000 ☐ $500 ☐ $100 ☐ $50 ☐ $25

Make checks payable to Clark for President.

Name _____

Address _____

City _____ State _____ Zip _____

Occupation _____

Business Address _____

BUSINESS REPLY MAIL

FIRST CLASS   PERMIT NO. 12388   WASHINGTON, DC

POSTAGE WILL BE PAID BY ADDRESSEE

CLARK
PRESIDENT
2300 Wisconsin Avenue, NW
Washington, DC 20007

NO POSTAGE
NECESSARY
IF MAILED
IN THE
UNITED STATES

record loses her own. Unmarried and childless persons must pay the same as people who want survivor insurance.

The elderly collecting benefits are harmed by the system's earnings test. This is the rule that retired persons lose one dollar in benefits for every two dollars earned over $4,000 a year. That's like a 50 percent tax on the marginal income. Clearly, this forces productive elderly people out of the labor market, imposing idleness and poverty on them and lost services on the rest of us.

The system harms all workers because their disposable income is reduced by the tax. This removes control over their lives since they are not permitted to apportion current and future spending according to their own values. Distant bureaucrats who think working people aren't smart enough to make decisions for themselves, make those decisions for them.

The system also harms the family. Before Social Security, younger members of families had a sense of responsibility to retired members. Social Security has taken this away by deceiving people into thinking the government takes care of old people when they retire. This has eroded an old and admirable virtue that will be recovered only when the government lets people take care of themselves and their own.

Finally, the Social Security system has devastating, hidden consequences for the economy, which means that everyone's ability to make a better life is greatly inhibited. Economists have known for some time that the system siphons off savings and capital investment, reducing economic growth and decreasing employment. The reason for all this is the pay-as-you-go principle. In private plans, collected premiums are invested in productive enterprises. This assures that benefits will be available to the policyholder later, and, more importantly for this discussion, it channels needed wealth to industries that serve consumers. This capital is used to expand factories, buy better machines and tools, create jobs, engage in research and development, and for other purposes that ultimately increase the welfare of people.

This does not happen with Social Security. Current payments are not invested; they are paid as benefits and consumed. The lost opportunities and jobs are unmeasurable but nonetheless real. The working poor and unemployed may not know their plight is caused by this system, but in these hidden ways it is.

Besides this, since the Social Security tax is perceived by people as forced savings, they tend to reduce real savings, withdrawing more money from productive investments. Martin Feldstein estimates that in 1971, Social Security reduced personal savings by $40 billion to $60 billion. (Actual personal savings was $61 billion.) In 1978, Social Security taxes totalled $106.2 billion. Much of that might have been invested had it been left to the judgement of the wage earners themselves.

The point is that the Social Security system is impoverishing us. At a time when everyone complains about the lack of productivity, capital shortage and sluggish industries, we can't afford to have the government withdrawing billions from the economy.

This has a direct bearing on the workers of America. Wages rise with labor productivity, and capital makes labor more productive. The capital not available for investment because of Social Security represents lost jobs and wage increases. Obviously, the poor are the principal victims of this process. Besides this, Social Security prevents *new* accumulations of capital (recall the trust funds that would be created) and raises interest rates to the holders of capital as it becomes more scarce. The upshot is that the system indirectly redistributes wealth from poor to rich!

As Peter Ferrara writes in his *Social Security and the Inherent Contradiction*, the system "is hurting most of all the poor who most need the higher benefits of the private system and who could help their children and grandchildren break out of poverty with the large amounts of assets they could leave to them."

The injustice of Social Security cries out for reform. Neither the individual worker nor the economy as a whole can tolerate it much longer. The system is collapsing under its own weight and it is bringing us all down with it. We must start removing it from our backs.

We can begin to move toward a new system based on voluntary, cooperative, decentralized market institutions instead of the current centralized and bureaucratic system. Under this new system, no person now in or near retirement will lose any of his or her expected benefits. Young workers will be able to earn better retirement benefits than Social Security would provide, and workers between 40 and 65 would get at least as much as they now expect.

The first major reform to be effected is the elimination of the payroll tax (the Social Security tax). The payroll tax is regressive, falling most heavily on lower-income workers. And as we have seen, it has devastating consequences for our economy, withdrawing billions of dollars from productive investment. The government now admits that Social Security has never been an insurance program, that a worker's payroll taxes do not go toward his own retirement, so there is no reason to maintain a separate tax for Social Security. We should fund Social Security out of general revenues like other government programs, and by cutting federal spending in other areas, we can avoid any tax increase.

We can begin to move away from the payroll tax by eliminating the hospital insurance portion of the tax first. This portion of the tax amounts to 2.6 percent on the employee's income, out of the total 13.3 percent tax (counting both employee and employer shares, both of which are ultimately paid by the worker). After eliminating this part of the tax, we can move the next year to eliminate the rest of the tax.

When we eliminate the payroll tax, we would also stop the accumulation of further benefits. Workers, no longer paying Social Security taxes, would then be able to invest in private retirement plans, which, as we have seen, would provide better retirement benefits. Workers now in their forties, fifties, and sixties could not start at this point putting their Social Security payments into a private plan and come out ahead of Social Security. However, we could reduce the burden of future taxpayers by ceasing to collect Social Security taxes from them, allowing them to invest that amount in private plans, and then reducing their Social Security benefits by the amount their private plan paid. They would end up with at least the same amount they now expect, and future taxpayers would be relieved of some of the growing burden of Social Security payments. (Of course, if these workers made very wise investment decisions, they might in fact come out ahead of Social Security, which would be so much the better.)

Workers in their forties, fifties, and sixties would come out even or a little ahead under this system, but workers now in their twenties and thirties would find themselves well ahead. If a young worker stopped paying his or her Social Security taxes to the government and began investing the same amount privately instead, he or she would end up with significantly more retirement income than Social Security would provide. Young workers would be able to expect much better retirement benefits—and they would be able to count on it, since a private investment firm, unlike the government, would be legally obligated to pay off its debts.

To insure that these private retirement plans would in fact pay the benefits we have projected, they should be exempt from taxes, much as individual retirement accounts (IRAs) are now. We should ease the current restriction on IRAs and allow workers to put their money in any investment they choose. The individual could make these investments on his own or they could be made on his behalf by banks, insurance companies, trust companies, pension plan managers, or other investment experts. Individuals should be able to receive the full, real, before-tax rate of return on their retirement investments. This would mean that money invested in a retirement plan should be exempt from federal income tax. In addition, individuals should not have to pay income tax on income earned by such investments. Profits earned by that percentage of a corporation's assets owned by retirement accounts should be exempt from corporate taxes, since these profits are really being earned by IRAs. Finally, of course, the retirement benefits paid to individuals should be tax-exempt, just as Social Security benefits are now.

For those few individuals who neglected to provide for their own retirement, normal welfare programs—and increasingly, under a revitalized economy, voluntary charitable organizations—could provide assistance.

The benefits of this reform would be many. The Social Security system would be saved from its presently imminent bankruptcy. Capital formation would be encouraged as billions of dollars would be invested in the productive private sector, creating business expansion and new jobs. Middle-aged workers would be able to invest their retirement payments in a more reliable fund than Social Security. Young workers would be able to count on significantly improved retirement benefits. As fewer and fewer people draw from Social Security, the burden on the taxpayers would be reduced. We would save Social Security from bankruptcy *without* increasing taxes.

Only a fundamental reform like this can avert the otherwise inevitable consequences of today's Social Security problems: higher taxes and bankruptcy. Any politician who says we don't need such fundamental reform is seriously irresponsible. The reform presented here is absolutely necessary. The liberty and prosperity of the American people depend on it.

CHAPTER 8:

Freeing Up the System

In mid-May, 1980, Miami's black community exploded in almost a week of bloody riots. Jesse Jackson and Andrew Young rushed to the scene to try to calm things down, and President Carter even considered going there himself. (Carter went to the State of Washington instead, apparently deciding that he would have more luck in trying to cool down the erupting Mt. St. Helens. His judgment was confirmed a few weeks later when he *did* go to Miami and was booed and jeered.)

Journalists everywhere were suddenly reminded of the nationwide riots of the late '60s, and of the Long Hot Summer of 1968. It became clear that twelve years of federal programs, under Democratic and Republican administrations alike, have *not* revitalized the inner cities. Nor have they diminished poverty or eliminated racial disharmony.

But the record of the Republicans and Democrats is worse than that. Under their rule, we have had more and more programs, spending more and more money, over a period of decades, and yet poor people have not realized the benefits usually associated with such large sums of money. Nor has the problem of poverty in our society diminished. Instead, we have been changing what was once a society of economic growth and opportunity into a society of stagnation and status. At the turn of the century, America, known throughout the world as a "beacon of hope," offered unparalled opportunities to poor and immigrants alike. It was a land where anyone could come, bringing with them all their possessions on their backs, and facing the vast opportunities for work and advancement which America offered, achieve within a few short years the kind of prosperity which was largely unknown throughout the rest of the world.

But things have changed. After decades of economic policies

adopted by the Democrats and Republicans, the world's fastest growing economy has ground to a halt. A vast number of government programs ostensibly designed to help the poor, to make the economy more efficient, to improve our lot and to promote economic growth, have produced precisely the opposite effect. Hundreds of billions of dollars have been wasted on social programs which have *not* helped the poor, but which instead have effectively kept them "in their place"—economically immobile and dependent. And meanwhile the government has sabotaged those elements of a free market economy which were once the best hope of all those who wanted a better way of life. We have seen government prattle on and on about helping the poor—and we have watched that same government slam the door on their future.

Who are the poor? They are elderly; they are woman-headed families of small children; they are fathers shut out of the job market; they are unemployed teenagers. Almost half of them are black, and *most of these* live in our devastated ghetto areas, where almost 25 percent of the federal domestic budget was spent in 1979. Is all this money bringing hope?

Quite the contrary. In the aftermath of the riots in Miami, *Newsweek* asked blacks if they thought that life in America is improving for blacks, and found that the number of people optimistic about their futures had dropped by a third since 1969. Half of today's respondents think things are improving—but in 1969, 75 percent thought so. *This* is where the policies of the Republican and Democratic parties have brought us. Facing an ever bleaker future, America's less fortunate citizens are finding themselves increasingly frustrated, threatened, and angry.

What we need is a new, radical alternative, so that the slammed door can be opened. The Republicans and Democrats have failed us, and their policies are only making things worse.

At a rally on April 29 in front of New York Governor Hugh Carey's office in Albany, black speakers asked, not for more government programs, but instead for *freedom* from government controls, controls which they justifiably see as making their own progress nearly impossible. One of the speakers denounced politicians as "thieves who take everything from the people and just give us welfare to keep us down."

In every society, there have been individuals who cannot look after their own needs. We've all been there—all human infants are totally dependent on the good will of others for their survival. The handicapped, the disabled, the elderly generally require help from others, too, and there are always people in need as a result of catastrophe: fire, flood, earthquake, hurricanes, tornadoes, drought. And in industrial societies you can add people who lose their jobs due to changes in economic conditions or their state of health.

But to make this fact of the human condition the excuse for decades of botched government policies and programs which create widespread dependency on government, spread poverty and despair like a blight, spawn a bloated bureaucracy, and dehumanize everything they touch, is simply unforgivable.

What have government programs done to eliminate poverty? Consider the record.

A composite of hundreds of central city areas, according to the *New York Times*, would look like this: "a land of several thousand square miles, of rubble-strewn streets and vacant blocks, abandoned stores, stripped-down hulks of automobiles, bleak and compacted public and private housing projects, battered school buildings, old men with glazed eyes."

The income of all blacks relative to whites reached its peak in 1969, a year before the federal government began insisting on the implementation of what UCLA economist Thomas Sowell calls "affirmative action mandatory quotas," and has declined ever since.

During roughly the same period, the income of families in our cities did not rise with inflation, although that of suburban families generally did. (There were more minority families, of course, in the cities than in the suburbs.) City income increased only by 57 percent; at the same time the Consumer Price Index went up 65 percent. This means that while the median family income in the central cities was 83 percent of that in the suburbs in 1969, eight years later it had fallen an average of 4 percentage points—and by more than that in some key areas. It had fallen from 72 percent to 60 percent in Atlanta, from 89 to 67 percent in Philadelphia, from 71 to 61 percent in New York, and from 72 to 63 percent in Cleveland. The proportion of black families with income below the poverty line was between 25 and 30 percent at the beginning of the past decade, and remains the same today. Despite considerable economic growth, poor people have been left behind.

And this is true despite the billions upon billions of dollars spent on "transfer" programs over the last decade—food stamps, rent subsidies, Medicaid—which have transferred money and services from taxpayers to the poor. In 1968 such programs totalled $56.5 billion. Ten years later they had been increased to a staggering $215.2 billion which, if it had actually gone to the poor, was enough to give more than $25,000 to each poor family of four. Obviously, it didn't all go to the poor.

According to the Census Bureau, there were 25.4 million poor people in the country in 1968, and there were still 24.7 million poor in 1978. In 1965, 28 percent of our people were poor; by 1977, hundreds of billions spent to aid them had resulted in a reduction of this figure by a mere one percent, to 27 percent. (Of course, the calculation of the number of poor people could be reduced by counting certain government services they receive; but this doesn't change the fact that such people are still trapped in the poverty cycle without jobs or any income of their own.)

Why has this happened? Why have hundreds of billions of dollars ostensibly spent on the poor not eliminated poverty?

The answer may be that these programs are in fact *not* primarily designed to help the poor. They are a political tool, a source of jobs for welfare workers, and a method of social control of the poor. Professors Frances Fox Piven and Richard A. Cloward, in their book *The Politics of Turmoil: Poverty, Race, & the Urban Crisis*, write, "The social-welfare agencies were legislated in the name of the poor, but the poor were not their true clientele."

The welfare system is really operated by and for its own bureaucracy. "The bureaucracies manipulate the benefits and services on which their clients come to depend in such a way as to control their behavior," Piven and Cloward write. The poor, who are forced onto welfare because the government's economic policies have destroyed millions of jobs, are controlled, interrogated, bullied, stigmatized, and dominated by bureaucrats. Welfare administrators investigate the "morals" of their tenants, employ their own police and quasi-judicial procedures, and carefully monitor the income of welfare recipients. Perhaps the most striking example of these practices is the midnight raid to see if mothers receiving welfare have a man on the premises. Is it any wonder that the poor begin to display the characteristics they are supposed to have? Denied any rights or dignity, finding their lives ruled by capricious and arbitrary regulations, they come to live in fear, acquiescing to the wishes of the bureaucrats.

Piven and Cloward suggest that the Great Society programs were designed not to help the poor but to further the political goals of the national Democratic Party. The new agencies were a way of bringing the federal government into direct contact with ghetto blacks, avoiding the necessity of going through Republican governors or anti-black Democratic city governments. The new federal offices in the ghetto—operating as delinquency-prevention, mental health, antipoverty, or model-cities agencies—were a modern-day version of the old-style political machine. They offered help in getting welfare and other public services. They hired neighborhood leaders as "community workers" to distribute patronage like the old ward heelers. Thus, Piven and Cloward say, "the national administration was revivifying the traditional strategy of urban politics: offering jobs and services to build party loyalty." When Nixon took office, he tried to change some of the rules: making more of the money go through state governments, for example, where Republicans had more control. The purpose was the same: using federal funds in the political interest of the party in power.

Who benefits most from these policies? Not the poor, obviously—they're still poor. The real beneficiaries are the social workers, planners, and welfare bureaucrats, along with the politicians who profit from the new political machines. If they actually helped people get off welfare and get jobs, the bureaucrats wouldn't be needed any more, and the politicians would lose a source of votes. It is in the interests of the bureaucrats and politicians to keep people poor.

Sam Brown, head of the government's ACTION agency which is responsible for many of these programs ostensibly designed to help the poor, recently admitted that "Despite our best intentions the government programs we have supported have unwittingly made the poor dependent and created a new bureaucratic and expert elite that too often denies poor people the opportunity to help themselves." One may question whether this outcome was really accidental, as Brown says, but there can be no doubt that the results are just as he says.

One major problem is that many regulators, bureaucrats, and social workers do not believe that poor people and neighborhood groups can solve their own problems. But for years Americans, including those in inner cities, have been finding their own solutions to community problems, without government help. Lately, however, government has often stepped in to outlaw these self-help activities.

In the mid-1960s Dr. Thomas Matthew, over the opposition of the New York City government, established a locally run hospital in the black section of Jamaica, Queens. He found, however, that public transportation there was inadequate for the patients and staff. Dr. Matthew purchased a few buses and established a regular, efficient, and successful bus service in Jamaica. The service was so successful that he established another line in Harlem. But Dr. Matthew did not have a city license to operate a bus service, and none was available. The city government went to court and shut down both bus lines.

A few years later Dr. Matthew and his colleagues took over an abandoned building in Harlem and established a low-cost hospital. The city government shut that down, too—it didn't meet regulations.

Another example: Black Philadelphians have had a long tradition of establishing their own nursing homes for the elderly, often under church auspices. Just a few years ago there were 25 such centers in Philadelphia's black neighborhoods. Then in 1974 the federal government adopted new nursing home regulations, setting up standards most of these facilities were unable to meet. As a result, almost all the nursing homes are now out of business.

Families across the country, particularly in the South, have traditionally "taken in" orphaned and abandoned children, caring for them in their homes. But state and county welfare agencies, insisting on a myriad of bureaucratic rules, have made these informal arrangements illegal in many cases.

In all these cases and more, government intervention has prevented people from solving their own problems. I think most people—black or white, rich or poor—are capable of making decisions and solving their problems if they're just given the chance. When Dr. Matthew was asked what the government could do to help blacks in New York, he replied, "Get out of our way, and let us try something." I think that's a good prescription for every level of government.

It's not surprising, then, that millions of people stay poor and dependent on government. For all the billions we have spent on "poverty" programs, we have not eliminated poverty.

But if we haven't healed the rift between black and white, or eliminated poverty, have we at least made strides toward providing the poor with what they need most—jobs? The fact is that Republican and Democratic programs have taken us in the opposite direction, sabotaging both jobs and those who need them. Herbert Hill, former labor secretary of the National Association for the Advancement of Colored People, is one of those who thinks that what we *have* accomplished is the creation of a permanently unemployed black underclass, and he makes the dire prediction that "virtually an entire generation of ghetto youth will never enter into the labor force."

Between 1967 and 1977, the black teenage population increased by 43 percent, while the white teenage population increased by only 18 percent. But during the same period, employment among white youth increased 29 percent, and only 7.7 percent among teenage blacks. In other words, there were more and more black kids, but jobs were going to their white counterparts. The August 1977 unemployment rate among black teenagers was more than 40 percent, as reported to President Carter in a report evaluating the results of his public jobs program, "a broad program to breathe life into urban centers where so many of the black unemployed live," according to the *New York Times*.

By the spring of 1979 the situation for minority youths was being compared to the depths of the Great Depression. Black leaders were beginning to believe that the unemployment rates, shocking as they were, didn't even begin to reflect the number of idle young blacks in ghettoes across the country. The *New York Times* discovered that in the 18 to 24 age group, more black youths were in local jails than in all the Federal public jobs programs put together.

So the public jobs programs which the Republicans and Democrats have offered as a sop to minorities have not done a thing to ease the problem of minority teenage and youth unemployment.

Consider the disastrous effects of these policies. The politicians have given us ruinous taxation policies. These high taxes have confiscated the capital which businesses would otherwise have been able to use to expand and create jobs. This has destroyed potential jobs and kept new businesses from being able to compete with established businesses, which are better able to absorb the tax burden. Particularly high city taxes have made these problems more acute in the cities and have driven countless businesses out of Northern cities to the suburbs or the Sunbelt. Instead of lowering taxes, the politicians complain about declining employment in the cities and raise taxes yet again. The result has been fewer and fewer manufacturing jobs for the urban poor.

Regulations of every sort have hampered businesses in the cities and destroyed countless more jobs. Benjamin Hooks, now head of the NAACP, once bought a doughnut shop in Memphis from a man who had owned it for 25 years. "In those 25 years, they had passed all kinds of laws," he recalls. "You had to have separate rest rooms for men and women, you had to have ratproof walls and everything on God's earth. We were hit with all those regulations, and they cost us $30,000. We had to close the shop." If an ambitious, gifted man like Ben Hooks couldn't survive the onslaught of regulations, what chance does the average aspiring entrepreneur have?

"It's obvious now," Hooks continues, "that nobody, but nobody, is buying into a decaying black ghetto except blacks themselves. So the effect of some regulations [like those described above] is almost 100% to exclude blacks."

The federal minimum wage law has destroyed hundreds of thousands of jobs for teenagers and minorities. The minimum wage law doesn't guarantee anyone a job at $3.10 an hour; it just makes it illegal for him to take a job that pays less. So the worker who at the moment isn't worth $3.10 an hour to an employer ends up with no job at all. Who is hurt most? Teenagers, of course, who haven't acquired many job skills. And especially minority teenagers, who have generally received a poor education in inner-city public schools.

But the minimum wage law doesn't only hurt teenagers. The teenager who can't get that first job soon becomes the young man or woman with no work experience, unable to get any job. And there will be unskilled adult workers who are not worth the minimum wage. So the potential employer decides to automate, or to hire one skilled worker instead of two or three unskilled workers, or to let his customers wait on themselves. Hundreds of thousands of jobs for the poor have been destroyed by this one piece of legislation—legislation framed by politicians who seem to think it's better to be on welfare than to hold down a low-paying job.

Professor Walter Williams, a Temple University economist with a special interest in minority problems, points out that black opportunities have in fact declined since the government made a commitment to improve the condition of minorities. In 1948, black teenage youth actually had a lower unemployment rate than whites of the same age. Dr. Williams is convinced that the tremendous rise in black unemployment is due to "the numerous laws that have the effect of reducing employment opportunities," and that the impact of minimum wage laws on black people is vastly underrated.

Certainly it is obvious by now to most free market economists, like Walter Williams and Thomas Sowell, that black unemployment has risen sharply with the increase and spread in scope of these minimum wage laws. But what is unusual is the number of opponents of the free market who have joined their ranks. Paul Samuelson, winner of the Nobel Prize in economics and a neo-Keynesian, is one; another is Gunnar Myrdal, a Nobel Prize-winning socialist economist, who talks about the effects of such laws on black unemployment in his indictment of the treatment of blacks in this country, *An American Dilemma*.

While the politicians have been driving people out of the labor market with minimum wage laws, preventing them from acquiring needed skills and experience, they have also been restricting employment opportunities by passing a blizzard of other laws, particularly licensing laws. Licensing laws limit entry into a profession, forcing potential workers to meet many cumbersome and often irrelevant criteria before they are licensed and allowed to work. Someone may be perfectly competent in construction work, as in carpentry or plumbing, in cutting hair, in driving a taxi, or any one of a vast number of other occupations, but unless he or she can obtain a license, all these skills amount to nothing

These laws are not designed to protect consumers. Rather they are framed by established interests to keep people out of the protected occupation, thus guaranteeing higher incomes for those who are already in the field. When licensing is introduced, often those who are entrenched in the occupation are automatically certified under a "grandfather" clause. And often the requirements for a license have nothing to do with ability to do the job—not because they are relevant to the job but because they limit entry into the field.

Further, many licensing examinations require that the applicants speak, read, and write standard English in order to answer the questions, regardless of whether this is relevant to practicing their trade among others who share the same dialect of non-standard English or of Spanish. This factor heavily discriminates against minorities, especially ghetto blacks and barrio Hispanics, who may be able to communicate perfectly with their potential customers.

Often entry is limited by artificial financial obstacles. Throughout American history, for example, immigrants and other ambitious Americans have made a living by peddling. Many peddlers have gone on to become successful, established merchants, in many cases the owners of department stores. Today, street vendors are a common sight in major cities. A poor person, unable to find a job or ambitious to go into business for himself, can become a street vendor with very little money. But in many cities established businesses have tried to use the government to run the vendors out of business. In Philadelphia the Chamber of Commerce supported a bill to require vendors to pay a $500 licensing fee. Such requirements in other cities keep many people out of the vending business.

A similar situation exists with regard to taxicabs. A young person who wanted to go into business for himself could buy a serviceable car for a relatively small amount—but in most major cities he could not use the car as a cab unless he purchased a certificate or medallion. In Miami, where black unrest has been most clear recently, such a certificate costs $15,000. In Chicago it's $40,000; in New York, $60,000. And those who already have certificates jealously guard their privilege. Recently the New York City Taxi & Limousine Commission held a public hearing on its proposal to increase the number of taxis in New York. Who showed up to testify? Representatives of the taxi industry and the driver's union—both in opposition to any increase in the number of taxis.

Not only do these laws deny the poor any opportunity to go into the taxi business, they have particularly hurt minorities. In cities with high license fees, there are fewer minority owner-operators than in the few cities without such fees.

And these laws have been growing at an astonishing rate, effectively leaving those who cannot meet arcane licensing requirements without a means of earning a living. By 1900, there were licensing laws limiting working in only two professions; by 1952, nearly 80 professions required licenses; but by 1980, the number of licensed occupations had risen to a startling figure of more than 800. All these laws simply prevent people from working when they are perfectly capable of doing so. They are designed to shut people out of the economic system—to slam the door in the face of those who want to succeed.

Over the years, Republicans and Democrats also have been adding to state and federal regulation of industry and to national labor laws, which has further reduced competition, harming minorities in devastating ways. I agree with Professor Williams when he says, "Market-entry regulations are *political* acts that have made it increasingly difficult for the black underclass to enter the mainstream of American society." To deprive people of the opportunity to work and to compete—to condemn them to a life on welfare—is, in my view, an outrage.

And, of course, while these bipartisan policies have been steadily restricting the availability of private sector jobs for minorities, a succession of public jobs programs has been unable to replace these lost jobs. When the Neighborhood Youth Corps and Operation Mainstream failed to solve the problems of youth unemployment, the Emergency Employment Act of 1971 budgeted $2 billion over two years. When that act expired, the Comprehensive Employment and Training Act (CETA) was passed in 1973, to train people for jobs at a cost of about $4,000 per person.

But when the Carter Administration committed $10 billion to public service jobs in 1977, claiming that these funds were especially aimed at "those most in need," primarily young blacks, the funds were administered by state and local governments which used the money instead to rehire personnel who had fallen victim to earlier payroll cuts—and untrained, inexperienced blacks were once again pushed aside.

Neither the Republicans nor the Democrats want to consider the real root of *this* problem, of course: the disaster of our government schools, which no longer educate—if they ever did—and are worst in the inner cities, of course. Bernard C. Watson, a black vice president of Temple University, located in the Philadelphia ghetto, says, "The education too many children receive in these classrooms is nothing short of a national scandal, an absolute disgrace."

Is it any wonder that more and more minority parents—deeply concerned about their children's future—are passionately searching for alternatives to the public schools? By 1976 it was estimated that more than 10 percent of the black children in Chicago went to Catholic schools—even though their families were predominantly Protestant. When the archdiocese of the Catholic Church in New York decided it could no longer keep a parochial school in a ghetto neighborhood open, the New York branch of CORE tried to buy it, so that hundreds of black children in the area might continue to have a better education than the local public schools provided

I have devoted an entire chapter to this education crisis, which isn't just an inner city crisis, or a black crisis. But because their options are more limited, inner city blacks are perhaps trapped most cruelly by the failure of our public schools. Blacks really do not need the extra handicap of schools that are unable to teach their captive students how to read and write.

Finally, there is the important area of housing. After more than 30 years of urban renewal programs, public housing programs, model cities programs, rent subsidies and rent controls, there is *less* housing for the poor than before these programs were begun. Urban renewal has destroyed three housing units for every one that was built, and over 70 percent of the families uprooted by this perverse program have been black.

Rent control laws have kept landlords from being able to make a profit on their buildings. Caught between rising taxes and virtually unchanging rents in a time of inflation, apartment owners find themselves unable to continue in business. They convert their buildings to condominiums or simply abandon them. Seeing the poor prospects for rental housing, potential entrepreneurs do not build new apartments. Shortages of rental housing develop, and the poor—who cannot afford to move to other cities or to buy condominiums—are hurt worst. The liberal Swedish economist Assar Lindbeck has said, "Rent control is the most effective method known for destroying a city, except for bombing." Building regulations have also prevented the construction of new housing units. Within a few more years, this crisis is likely to get much worse—and neither Republicans nor Democrats have proposed any policies that would allow the crisis to be forcefully met.

The plain fact is that we must rethink the entire approach of the two parties which have for too long dominated American politics. The government programs fastened upon us by Republicans and Democrats at all levels of government have made the poor worse off, not better. They have managed to throw

96

a few welfare bones at the disillusioned and oppressed victims of their policies. They have not only slammed the door on the future for many people, but have actually nailed the door of opportunity shut.

What can we do instead? What is the Libertarian alternative? Quite simply, we should free up the system.

We should free up the cities from the staggering burden of regulations and taxes. We should repeal rent control, zoning laws, and obsolete building codes, promoting the investment in new housing that the cities so desperately need. We should eliminate victimless crime laws, and put our police on the job of enforcing laws against crimes *with* victims, like mugging, robbery, rape, and murder—which are a blight on the lives of city dwellers, and especially those who live in our inner cities.

We should promote economic growth, which is the only hope of the poor for advancement and better lives in the future, by slashing taxes and deregulating the economy. Freeing our economy from government red tape and controls will find new investment flooding into the cities, new businesses being started by the less-well off, more jobs being created—meaningful jobs, not government make-work jobs which merely perpetuate the bureaucracies and lead to dead-ends for the poor.

We should begin to dismantle the welfare state, with its controls and regulations and manipulation, and make it possible for those now on welfare to make easier transitions into the labor market, ending the permanent cycle of dependency, subjugation, suspicion, and poverty.

We should free up our education system, abolishing compulsory attendance laws, and establish a system of tax credits for education, which will lead to freedom of choice in education, and competition among schools to see which education methods work best in educating our children.

We should abolish the minimum wage laws and licensing laws so that people can once again be free to compete and to work, so that no bureaucrat or politician backed by special interests can ever again stand between a human being and a chance to work for a living, bringing with it the dignity of self-reliance, not the dehumanizing dependency of helpless poverty and unemployment.

We can take a first step in this direction by establishing "enterprise zones" in many cities. In urban areas with unemployment rates double the national average, we should eliminate all controls, restrictions, and taxes to encourage the establishment of businesses and creation of jobs. We should eliminate zoning restrictions and building codes, which prevent innovative and changing land use; rent controls, which lead to the abandonment of buildings; minimum-wage laws, which prevent the employment of those who need jobs most; and all sorts of business regulations, which interfere with production and make it very difficult to establish new, small businesses. We should suspend property and business taxes, and maybe even personal income and social security taxes.

In short, we should remove all the taxes and controls which prevent the establishment of businesses and destroy jobs. At the same time, no business in an enterprise zone should be eligible for any government subsidy, grant, loan, loan guarantee, or other financing. We want real productive businesses, not companies dependent on the government. All these conditions must be absolutely guaranteed for a specified period of time—at least ten years. Otherwise entrepreneurs will be unwilling to start businesses because they will fear that taxes and regulations might suddenly be reimposed.

An enterprise zone policy will restore the economic vitality of our inner cities. Businesses will be established, jobs will be created, buildings will be refurbished and rebuilt. Once again our inner cities will be thriving, bustling centers of activity. Perhaps the most important benefit will be moral: inner-city residents will know that their own efforts can accomplish something; they will be able to build their own communities. Our cities will have a future of jobs, production, and opportunity.

These solutions are at once sweeping and simple. They are sweeping because they are radical in the true sense of that term: they go to the root of our problems, offering genuinely new solutions to the decades-old stagnation and failure which have been the hallmark of Republican and Democratic party policies. They are simple because they are grounded in principle: the principle of individual liberty, which holds that individuals know what's best for them, and when set free to act, can solve their own problems better than any impersonal and inhumane bureaucracies.

As Roy Fauntroy, a leader of the Southern Christian Leadership Conference, told a Miami rally in June, 1980, "The issue is justice. The problem is government. And the solution is in the hands of the people here."

Our current policies have not worked. They have devastated the poor, whose confusion, helplessness, dependence and rage increase daily. We now have but one choice: either the poor will remain at the bottom of our society, without a future, without dreams, without hope—or we can free up the system, and set people free—to work, compete, build, plan, and live. That is the *only* way to solve the problem of poverty and stagnation in this country. We must turn our backs on the policies which have failed, and make a fresh start.

CHAPTER 9:

With Liberty and Justice for All

In the minds of many of those who have heard something about libertarianism—which is a gratifyingly growing number of people—there is often a feeling that our philosophy stands above all for civil liberties and personal freedoms. In fact, the very word "libertarian" is sometimes used to signify a believer in complete freedom of choice in personal affairs for peaceful (sometimes called "consenting") adults. As I have tried to show throughout this small book, libertarianism is actually a much broader political position than that; it stands on a foundation of peaceful economic exchange and peaceful international relations as well.

But there is some truth in the widespread identification of our philosophy with basic civil and personal liberties. For one thing, no other political movement puts as much emphasis on these liberties as we do. To us it is self-evident that an individual has the right to speak his own mind and to do what he wishes with his own body, so long as he respects the equal right of others; and that the alternative to this view is, not to put too fine a point on it, slavery of one degree or other. That a woman should be forced to carry a pregnancy to term (assuming even that she can be forced to do so), or that any individual should be dictated to regarding what materials he may read or what substances he may ingest, strikes us as an obvious outrage against individual dignity.

It is true that some advances have been made in this whole area of personal and civil liberties in the recent past. But there are disturbing signs that a reaction has now set in against a relative loosening up of repressive rules. Besides—since we are Americans and really ought not to be satisfied with scraps thrown to us by our rulers—we must be clear that the progress that *was* made always fell far short of the ideal of a free society.

So it is not only a question of defending recent gains; we must go beyond them, and wrest freedoms away from a government that in many fields still claims to run the personal lives of its citizens.

The idea that personal and even civil liberties are under attack in the United States today will strike some people as far-fetched. We Americans love to sit back, especially on patriotic occasions like the Fourth of July, and listen to our leaders congratulate us on being "the freest nation on earth." We love to revel in the self-satisfaction of believing that our basic freedoms are guaranteed beyond any possibility of erosion. Don't we, after all, have our Bill of Rights, and our Supreme Court to act as the watch-dog of those rights?

But, as far as our civil liberties are concerned, the ominous fact is that over the past few years some of the most basic of them *have* indeed been eroded; and often the process has been abetted by the Supreme Court itself. Time and again the present Burger Court has acted to restrict freedom of the press—as working journalists have reason to know. In 1978, for instance, in *Zurcher v. Stanford Daily*, the Court legitimized police ransacking of homes and offices of *anyone*—even those suspected of no crime whatsoever—in cases where it was believed evidence might exist of crimes committed by others. In the notorious *Snepp* case, the Court gave federal agencies unprecedented powers over employees who might be tempted to blow the whistle on what they saw going on within their agencies—who might place their obligation to the public above loyalty to a department. These are only two examples of a trend which many knowledgeable observers, such as Nat Hentoff, have come to see as almost a vendetta against freedom of the press on the part of the present Court.

Other infringements of journalistic freedom are of longer standing. Thus, the Federal Communications Commission (FCC) continues to bedevil electronic newspeople with its Byzantine "fairness doctrine" and "equal time provision," helping in its own little way to keep much of radio and television a flat, intellectually desolate wasteland.

The Federal Election Commission, a more recent innovation, interferes with free speech in political campaigns. The

FEC limits individual contributions to political candidates to $1,000, so the person who wants to advance his ideas through the political process has severe restraints placed on him. The FEC gives taxpayers' money to Republican and Democratic candidates for their campaigns, while it prevents independents and new-party candidates from receiving either government funding *or* sufficient private funding. Of course, I don't think taxpayers should be taxed to support candidates they don't approve of, and I wouldn't accept taxpayer financing if it was offered. But my campaign is subject to severe contribution limits and cumbersome reporting requirements, which are a greater burden to independent and new-party campaigns than to the established parties. Is it any wonder that a law passed by Republicans and Democrats in Congress serves to protect Republicans and Democrats from new competition?

Some government agencies are even more predatory in their attacks on our basic freedoms. No one who reads the newspapers is unaware of the depredations of the FBI and CIA in the not-so-distant past. The story of the FBI's COINTELPRO program, the CIA's aptly named CHAOS program (for *domestic* spying—in direct contravention of its charter), and many similar cases has been brought together in one volume recently by Frank Donner, in his *Age of Surveillance*. These various programs and plans have amounted to a whole system of repressing and disorganizing political dissent in the United States.

Often the spying and harassment of citizens by agencies whose alleged purpose is to protect our rights seem something abstract and almost unreal to many of us. But once in a while what has been done to us becomes frighteningly real. In August 1979 the talented actress Jean Seberg committed suicide. It was then learned that, starting in 1970, when she was pregnant, the FBI had spread the false story that the father of her child was a member of the Black Panthers, to discredit her. This lingering slander so demoralized Ms. Seberg, according to her friends, that finally she put an end to her life. Earlier, as is now known, the FBI had attempted to drive Martin Luther King, Jr., to suicide, by threatening to make public some tapes

102

allegedly containing information on his sex life. The inevitable question arises, has it come to *this* in America?

If the story of the war on dissenters waged by the federal intelligence agencies is, by now, a rather familiar one, there is another agency in Washington whose activities liberals, sadly, have not been as quick to expose. This agency operates, for all practical purposes, totally outside of the law in its dealings with the citizens. The world in which it lives and moves and has its being is one that is rather alien to Americans, and has recently been described by journalist Blake Fleetwood:

> It is a land ruled by Draconian laws. There people are guilty until proven innocent. Even when you've done nothing wrong, it is wiser to confess and pay a large fine than to hire a lawyer to establish your innocence. Agents of this regime routinely seize homes, businesses, cars, bank accounts—even before the victims are told what they have been accused of. The incomprehensible laws change all the time. . . ; when new laws are made the regime won't disclose them to the citizens. . . . If they feel like it, they can prosecute you for doing exactly what they told you to do. And if the regime is after you, there's nothing it won't stoop to: It will bug phones, pick locks, hire women to prostitute themselves, and use a variety of methods to spy on your private life.

This lawless regime is the Internal Revenue Service (IRS), and the well-documented indictment I have quoted from appears, not in any wild-eyed publication of the lunatic fringe, but in the staid and sober *Saturday Review*. Mr. Fleetwood, who has written for the *New York Times* and other newspapers, adds that the IRS "has been asking for more money and sweeping new powers from Congress to clamp down on anti-tax behavior."

By now it should be manifest to everyone that the IRS is an institution which could fit much more comfortably into the "legal" order of the Soviet Union than into our own society With the tax revolt sure to spread in the coming years, all we can expect from the IRS is still more blatant disregard for our basic rights to liberty and property, ever more outrageous high-handedness in exacting its levies. That's why I support the Taxpayer's Bill of Rights currently being considered by Congress and actively promoted by the National Taxpayers Legal Fund chaired by Eugene McCarthy.

But the mania to control extends far beyond even our civil liberties in the narrower sense. It is rampant everywhere—from drugs and "pornography," to consensual sexual relations, to guns and mandatory helmet laws, to saccharin, laetrile, and even vitamin dosages. It seems that as soon as people discover something they want to do, the bureaucrats will be there, armed and ready to monitor, supervise, guide, ration, license, prohibit—or else, if they're feeling particularly generous—merely to tax it. And everywhere they have their little would-be ayatollahs—of the left or right—to egg them on.

One of the most egregious examples of government paternalism is the so-called war on drugs, which has been going on for decades now, and has cost taxpayers many billions of dollars. It is one of the most preposterous frauds ever imposed on the American people. Or, more precisely, it is the worst fraud inflicted on us since the "noble experiment" of Prohibition, which ended so ignominiously in 1933. The parallels between the old alcohol prohibition and the new drug prohibition are so obvious you would think they could penetrate even the smokescreen of deliberate obfuscation generated by the thousands of bureaucrats who now have a vested interest, in power and money, in the war. Just as with the prohibition of alcohol, drug prohibition, is, first of all, an insolent interference on the part of the politicians in the personal choices of individuals; and, second, an interference that, even from the viewpoint of the prohibitionists, results in much more harm than good.

What is more evident than that you have a right to put whatever substances you choose into your own body? The contrary view—that the government has various rights over your body, even in the absence of an injury to the rights of others—is, to be sure, a conceivable position; but it pertains, logically, to a different kind of social order than the one we Americans have selected for ourselves. We all correctly see alcohol prohibition as an attempt by some segments of our society to impose their own cultural norms on other segments. Similarly, drug laws are nothing more than an attempt to dictate what some people may ingest for recreational purposes, by other people who happen to prefer gin, Scotch, tea, postum, or Chablis.

Moreover, the drug laws have had an even greater effect than Prohibition in encouraging crime. It was no accident that Prohibition was the age of the great gangsters, and a time of "primitive capital accumulation" for the big crime families. By the same token, it is no accident that, under the aegis of our drug laws, our cities have become the stalking-grounds for the users of certain drugs who must pay ridiculously exorbitant prices to support their habits. The time is coming when we will have to choose between imposing our norms for intoxicants on a large portion of the population, and having cities we can live in.

But so fanatical has the crusade against drugs become, so merciless and vindictive are the crusaders, that it seems there are no lengths to which they will not go. The following is from an item in the *Washington Post* for December 14, 1979; it is by no means a unique example:

> Virginia Gov. John N. Dalton has granted a conditional pardon to Robert E. Moore, a quadriplegic who was sentenced in 1977 to 21 years in prison for selling $25 worth of marijuana and sleeping pills . . . Moore's pardon was conditioned on his serving one year of the 21-year sentence, paying a $1,000 fine and submitting to 10 years of supervision by the State Parole Board . . . Dalton's action does not mean automatic pardons for other Virginia prisoners serving long sentences for the sale of marijuana . . . There are several persons serving sentences in excess of 20 years in Virginia prisons for selling marijuana under an earlier state law . . .

Does this mean that we Libertarians do not believe drug-taking is harmful? Of course it can be harmful—much like many other things that different people choose to do in their lives. One thing that freedom indubitably means is the right to go to hell—or heaven—in your own way.

The Libertarian Party is the first to propose a solution to the fine drug mess the government has gotten us into. It is individual freedom—and individual responsibility. Taking drugs—like using pornography, or patronizing prostitutes—is a matter best left to personal choice, with the person assuming responsibility for the consequences of his choice, whatever they may be.

It is a cause for wry amusement, or else for deep discouragement, depending on your temperament, to see the logical contortions some politicians go through when it comes to issues like drugs or pornography. This is especially true of conservative politicians such as Ronald Reagan. Their problem is particularly acute, since they purport to be the special champions of free enterprise and individual rights. They bemoan the fact that property rights are under increasing attack from government bureaucrats, and they—quite correctly—cite the actions of the IRS, OSHA, EPA, and other government bureaucracies to prove that our individual freedoms are at the moment fighting a losing battle with state power. But, just as they ignore the abuses of alphabet agencies that happen to be engaged in political surveillance, such as the CIA and FBI, so they fall into a grave-like silence when it is a question of assaults on freedom by the notorious Drug Enforcement Administration (DEA). But the simple question these conservatives—and all of us—must face up to is this: Why is the marijuana a drug dealer imports from Columbia any less private property than the Sonys a television dealer imports from Japan? And isn't the inventory of a pornographer just as much his property as another person's shares of AT&T? In the Libertarian view, private property—much like liberty itself—is an indivisible concept. It either holds for everyone, or else ultimately it will hold for no one.

Recently, one of the most widely discussed topics in this whole area of personal liberties has been the rights of homosexuals. Since we favor individual freedom, it goes without saying that Libertarians favor complete equal rights for gay people. The time has come to recognize that homosexual men and women, by nature, possess the same rights that all other men and women do. This implies, among other things, an end to all laws that make crimes of voluntary homosexual acts; an end to police harassment and persecution of gays, an everyday affair throughout most of the country; the end of discrimination by the increasingly arbitrary Immigration and Naturalization Service (INS) against gays desiring to enter the United States; and the end of discrimination against homosexuals in the Armed Services, as well as other government positions.

Many persons will object that this last proposal, which includes permitting homosexuals to teach in the public schools, violates the rights of others—namely of parents who have moral qualms against such teachers being in contact with their children. Although I recognize the problem, I am afraid that *at this point* there is nothing that can be done about it. If there were parents who objected to their children being taught by teachers married to spouses of another race, this would not constitute sufficient grounds to exclude members of mixed marriages from teaching positions. The law must be even-handed; sexual preference is not a factor it ought to consider.

I have said that "at this point" there is nothing that can equitably be done to accomodate those parents who object (mistakenly, in my view) to homosexual teachers. It should be obvious that the real problem here, as in so many other cases, is the involvement of government; and the withdrawal of government from the business of education would defuse the conflict. As Libertarians, we favor maximizing *voluntary* as against *coerced* interactions among people. But that implies that people should be free not only to associate with others, but *not* to associate with them, as well. Thus, we strongly oppose any legislation forcing the individual who is prejudiced against gay people to employ them in a private business, rent or sell an apartment or house to them, or allow them into his establishment. In particular, private schools should be free to make whatever rules they wish on the subject. Just as it is absurd for the law to interfere in the private sexual relations of homosexuals, or to harass them in their places of recreation, so it is absurd for the law to compel Catholic, Baptist, or other religious schools to employ teachers whom they happen to consider notorious sinners. Again, as the reader will note, Libertarians propose solutions that cut across the usual liberal and conservative lines.

It is time for us finally to grow up as a people, and acknowledge that sexual preferences are not something that should concern the law. America is not one great socialist commune—some kind of super-Cuba—where we collectively decide on our preferences in sex or intoxicants, and then impose that decision on everyone. America is millions upon millions of quite diverse individuals and families, who must be accorded the right to pursue their own lifestyles in peace, so long as they accord peace to everyone else.

Does this mean that Libertarians have no personal standards in these matters? Of course not, no more than favoring freedom of religion implies an absence of personal religious beliefs. Do Libertarians believe that parents who are worried about the influence of pornography or drugs on their child are silly old Neanderthals who should be urged to "get with it"? Not at all. I am myself a parent, and my wife and I are just as concerned about bad influences on our son as most parents are. Our Libertarian viewpoint in no way interferes with our guiding our child in these matters, firmly if need be. We happen personally to agree with the Libertarian psychiatrist, Dr. Thomas Szasz, who has said that one of the scandals in our contemporary society is that children are treated as adults, while adults are treated as children. Clearly, a child requires a sense of values and moral standards that will enable him to make intelligent, decent, and life-enhancing choices for himself. These values and standards must ultimately come, for the most part, from the family, and from the other influences—church, temple, school, and so on—that the family chooses to have collaborate in the rearing of the child. What we object to is the state's growing assertion of control, not only over the rearing of children, but over the actions of adults as well. The right place for paternalism—and maternalism—is in the home, not in government.

It is a sad fact that the word "family" has been degraded into a code word. It is a code word, well-understood by those who cynically use it, for suppression of the rights of individuals. Ideally, the family should be the seed-bed of self-reliant, self-respecting persons as concerned with the rights of others as with their own. But the hawkers of "family" as a political slogan mean to set it in opposition to the rights of women who want to control their own reproductive lives, of users of pornography, of homosexuals, and of others.

The institution of the family is a hardy plant, one that has evolved through its history. If its future evolution is left to the free choice and contractual agreement of the people involved, it is hard to imagine the family ever disappearing. We don't have to have a government "family policy"; like religion, the family is one of those institutions that can very safely be left to the voluntary sector of society.

To those who are worried about threats to the future of the family, I would say, don't look in the direction of the women's movement, and women's struggle for equal worth—look in the direction of the legions of government agencies that have, one after another, usurped the functions and duties that used to be a part of family life. And don't worry so much about gay people serving as a "bad example" to your children—worry rather about the public school administrators who feel they have the state-given right to indoctrinate your children in whatever advanced and enlightened ideas they pick up from the magazines they read.

For those who morally disapprove of some social innovation or other, there are numerous measures that can be taken. The simplest is to refuse to associate with persons of whose actions you disapprove. Another, and often very effective, measure is the boycott. It is an eminently Libertarian means of protest, since it consists in the voluntary withdrawal of patronage. The organization known as Women Against Violence Against Women, for example, has found the boycott of great value in their campaign to stop record companies and other firms from portraying women in a humiliating manner, which WAVAW holds encourages sexism and the abuse of women; it has chosen this route, rather than the easier one of advocating censorship. Other feminist organizations have promoted a boycott of travel to states that have not yet ratified the Equal Rights Amendment. On the other side, various religious groups have undertaken boycotts of sponsors of television programs they consider too violent or sexually oriented. There is nothing in all this inconsistent with the Libertarian position. On the contrary. Boycotts and peaceful protests are ways of making your own values known; and they can lead to the initiation of dialogue and negotiations among conflicting groups, opening up minds and possibly producing compromises. They are in a different world altogether from calling in the cops to make sure that your side is victorious.

The women's movement has pointed us in the right direction on many of these issues. I think the essence of the women's movement is the demand that women be treated as individuals, with the same rights and opportunities as men. Women have worked to end the sexist laws that prevent them from holding certain jobs, that deny them equal inheritance rights, that refuse them equal access to the courts. Laws that were passed ostensibly to "protect" women have in fact limited their job opportunities and kept them out of the economic mainstream.

I support the Equal Rights Amendment because it would sweep away these laws. It would prohibit government discrimination against women—or men—on account of their sex. If interpreted properly, ERA will not interfere with private, voluntary activities, with businesses or private schools or home life. It will forbid the *government* from discriminating against some of its citizens. To those who worry that ERA will require that women be subject to any new draft, I say let us have *no* draft, for either men or women.

The activities of the women's movement in demanding that women be treated as individuals, in proclaiming the right of women—and men—to pursue any career they choose, in working for a society based on freedom, equality, and individualism, are essentially libertarian. Like them, Libertarians seek a society in which all people have the opportunity to achieve their own goals.

I have enough faith in progress to believe that some day, perhaps in the not-too-distant future, people will look back on our age in bewilderment, as we look back on the age of religious wars and persecution in Europe. On the one hand, so

110

much intellectual eminence, such creativity in so many fields. On the other hand, even many of the best minds seemed incapable of grasping the simple idea that opposing religions could live together in peace. Sometimes the failure to grasp the idea led to attempts to exterminate those with conflicting views; always the state power was called upon to weigh the competition on one side or the other.

In the same way, we appear to feel that varying lifestyles cannot be tolerated within our great and complex American society—that the state power must come down with full force on those who are different, or else chaos will ensue. History demonstrates how false this view was with regard to religious dissenters; I believe that the future will show how false it is in the case of our own dissenters who wish to pursue their happiness in their own way.

CHAPTER 10:

The Politics of Manipulation

Six months before the November, 1980 elections, the Republican nomination apparently his for the taking, Ronald Reagan let it be known in the news media that his campaign would portray him as a "flexible moderate" in his race against his Democratic opponent.

The words "flexible moderate" could apply equally well to the incumbent, Jimmy Carter, or to John B. Anderson, running as an Independent, as they are portrayed by their campaigns.

In fact, all over the country, Republican, Democratic, and most Independent candidates for offices ranging from state legislature to the U.S. Senate, are in a mad scramble to portray themselves as "flexible moderates." One can almost envision scrapping the Republican and Democratic labels, merging these parties with Independents like Anderson, and creating one grand Flexible Moderate Party which will carry its banner in future elections against, presumably, the Inflexible Immoderate Party.

Such a scenario is not that farfetched, for the fact is that, once the nominations are won and the intra-party bloodletting is over, the victorious nominees start moving toward the center, whitewashing whatever few meaningful statements they might have made in the heat of the primaries, and covering up whatever might be protruding in the way of principle or strongly-held opinions with a coat of mush.

The "flexible moderate" candidate pins his hopes of victory on the prospect of getting a plurality of the voters to decide that he's not as bad as the other candidates in the field. Such a candidate doesn't care why people vote for him; a vote cast for the "lesser of two (or three) evils" counts as much as a vote cast out of enthusiastic support. And the eventual winner will surely claim a "mandate from the people" after the votes are counted and victory is in hand.

This is the Politics of Manipulation. This is the politics which insists that principles, ideas, and issues don't matter nearly so much as image, style, and affability.

As contemptible as this kind of politics is, it is only one side of the 1980 presidential campaign. The other side is the brazen attempt by Carter, Reagan, and Anderson to promise special favors and special treatment to various groups of voters in return for their support. They do this in the full realization that government action on behalf of one special interest or voting bloc will necessarily require some other group in society to pick up the tab. When Ronald Reagan promises a group of corporate executives that his administration will keep their corporations strong . . . when Jimmy Carter tells a gathering of government employees that their jobs, pay raises, and benefits are safe and secure with him . . . when John Anderson, before an audience of public school teachers, vows that federal aid to education will be a cornerstone of his administration . . . they are, in effect, doing nothing less than attempting to buy votes with money that belongs to other people—the American taxpayers.

This, too, is the Politics of Manipulation, the kind of politics which views voters not as individual thinking *persons*, but as faceless units in voting blocs who can be had for the price of a promise and a smile.

The Politics of Manipulation is a truly vicious cycle of blurred images, soft faces, hollow forms, and empty promises. After the whirling and spinning stops, all members of society—rich and poor, young and old, white and nonwhite—find they have a still greater burden to bear.

Reagan, Carter, and Anderson are all willing participants in the Politics of Manipulation. A look behind the carefully cultivated images of "flexible moderates," an attempt to penetrate the curtain of promises to find the substance of their policies and programs—reveals more similarities than differences among the three candidates.

Ronald Reagan, despite his shifts to the center, is considered a "conservative," although his record as governor of California indicates a ready willingness to increase public spending in the manner of—you guessed it—a "flexible moderate." On economic issues, Reagan is considered to be oriented toward the free market, and his stated positions on these issues do sometimes bear superficial resemblance to Libertarian positions. Reagan favors a balanced federal budget, as do I, but he is unclear as to the level of taxing and spending at which his budget would be balanced.

Early in the campaign for the Republican nomination, *U.S. News and World Report* asked Reagan and the other candidates if they would cut federal spending and, if so, where they would make cuts. Reagan's answer was virtually identical to that of the other candidates: "I would cut the rate at which spending increases."

Cutting the *rate of increase* is not the same as cutting spending, and Reagan knows it. If federal spending is scheduled to increase from $600 billion this year to $700 billion the next, then cutting next year's budget to $650 billion cuts the rate of increase, but it does not cut spending—it still increases it. Therefore, to achieve a balanced budget, tax revenues also must increase, not only to match the increase in spending, but also to cover the existing deficit. Balancing the budget at a higher level can mean only that tax revenues are increased.

But Reagan says he wants to lower taxes. Reagan supports the Kemp-Roth tax cut proposal, which would cut tax rates 30 percent for individuals and corporations over a three-year period, 10 percent each year. Note, however, that it applies to tax *rates*, not total dollars. If you paid 30% of your income to the federal government this year, then, under Kemp-Roth, you would pay 27% the next year. Of course, if your pay increased next year to meet or exceed the rate of inflation, the total amount you pay in taxes to the federal government would increase, since you would likely find yourself in a higher tax bracket, and Social Security taxes are scheduled to rise. Only if your income stayed exactly the same from year to year would the dollar amount of your taxes be likely to decrease—and this would be small comfort indeed to someone whose income is being eaten away by double-digit inflation.

On the issue of inflation, Reagan correctly perceives that

a balanced federal budget would be a significant step toward removing the temptation to increase the supply of money and credit—creating cheaper dollars—to cover the budget deficit. Having gone this far, however, he stops, apparently unwilling to identify the sole source of inflation as the expansion of the supply of money and credit, and equally unwilling to state his intention of stopping this expansion by cutting the actual levels of federal spending. For him to do so would be to admit that the federal government alone causes inflation, which is not a becoming position for a "flexible moderate" to take.

Reagan proposes to balance the budget, lower taxes, and reduce inflation—yet there is one key plank in the Reagan platform which by itself, if carried out, would thoroughly demolish these good intentions and render their successful implementation impossible.

I refer to Reagan's policy on military spending and foreign affairs. Unlike most of his positions on domestic issues, Reagan is crystal clear on this point: he will increase the military budget; he will build new weapons systems; he will expand our military presence overseas; and he will "get tough" with the rest of the world, our allies and our enemies alike.

What are the implications of such a position? On the domestic front, it guarantees a substantial hike in federal spending . . . in a budget which Reagan claims will be balanced, with lower individual tax rates. To incorporate a huge military spending increase into a budget balanced even at the present level will also require domestic spending slashes in other portions of the budget. This, in turn, will require Congress to sacrifice billions of dollars in pet domestic programs set up to enhance their re-election, a trade-off they're unlikely to make given the fact that Reagan would merely be rearranging spending priorities, not making significant across-the-board cuts. The odds, then, greatly favor the proposition that a Reagan administration, placing its priorities on actual increases in the military budget, will preside over a vastly increased total budget. The pressure to increase spending on all budget items will force Reagan either to approve a huge budget deficit—thus fueling inflation—or to balance the budget at levels much higher even than at present, resulting in a huge general tax increase.

The real problem in the Reagan approach to spending—favoring military expenditures, seeking to cut back other programs—is that it is "shuffling deck chairs on the Titanic." What Reagan and other traditional politicians fail to realize is that the United States is heading for economic disaster because the level of federal spending is far too high, not because certain departments of government have relatively more to spend while other departments have relatively less.

Increased military spending would do more than increase the pressures favoring higher taxation and inflation. It will create an economic climate approaching that of wartime, in which favored businesses and industries reap huge profits from taxpayer dollars funneled through to them by the Pentagon. Even now, many large corporations owe their very existence to government contracts, the sloppy administration of which permits cost overruns in the millions and billions of dollars, and which guarantee their position of dominance in the marketplace. Such contracts create a continuing dependence upon increased federal spending—and the greatest tragedy is the dependence upon government fostered among the individual employees of these corporations and their families. Such a situation—which Reagan's policies can only intensify—is the very opposite of a free market economy in the Libertarian sense. It only tightens the grip of the "military-industrial complex" which Dwight Eisenhower warned us about twenty years ago, and it only increases the certainty that newer, smaller businesses which seek only the equal opportunity to compete in a free economy will be no match for an established corporation whose life-blood is a succession of fat government contracts. Higher levels of military spending translate into a greater level of welfare for the rich, and a greater degree of dependence and economic immobility for other segments of society.

But more than a likely increase in the overall level of taxing and spending . . . more than another step toward a permanent dependence on the corporate state . . . . the Reagan military and foreign policy, with its belligerence and threats, constitutes a real, constant danger both to peace and security. I've already discussed the Libertarian view of what a proper foreign policy should be; it's sufficient to say that Reagan's view is its polar opposite, carrying the concept of interventionism to an extreme which is truly frightening in a nuclear age.

My examination of Reagan's policies will conclude with a look at his record as governor of California. Just as the federal budget has doubled every eight years under Republicans and Democrats alike, so too did Reagan's budget double during his eight years as governor. Just as Republican and Democratic administrations have sought to hide or cushion the reality of our ever-increasing tax burden, so too did Governor Reagan cave in to the pressure to institute the first withholding tax in California history. Just as traditional politicians have always held little respect for basic civil liberties, so too has Reagan demonstrated little sympathy for peaceful dissent, alternative lifestyles, or other aspects of non-aggressive personal behavior which may differ from the social norm.

A Reagan administration is a disaster waiting to happen. Let's turn now to a disaster which has already happened.

Jimmy Carter may well be the first incumbent president in history to seek re-election on the slogan, "If at first you don't succeed, try again." His central campaign strategy of painting his opponents as dangerous and irresponsible appeals only to those voters who are convinced that they must choose among "the lesser of three evils," and plunges the Politics of Manipulation to a new low.

Carter's record in office is a textbook example of all of the evils and flaws in the present political structure—and an equally compelling illustration of why America needs to move in a new direction.

Carter won the 1976 election, in part, on a promise to balance the budget and streamline the federal government. He has done neither. In four years he has run up cumulative federal deficits of $209 billion, including off-budget items. The budget itself has skyrocketed 52 percent since 1977, from $402 billion to the fiscal 1981 level of at least $612 billion. Even if you take into account inflation since 1976, federal tax receipts have increased $125 billion in 1981 dollars.

Far from streamlining government, Carter has created two mammoth new federal departments at cabinet level: the Department of Energy, with 21,054 employees and a budget of $8.7 billion, and the Department of Education, with 7000 employees and a budget of $13.5 billion. To be sure, the Department of Education was broken away from the Department of Health, Education, and Welfare (now the Department of Health and Human Services)—but the added cost of having two departments instead of one has been about $2 billion.

Carter's proposals for the fiscal 1981 budget—which he labeled "prudent and responsible"—in fact will impose a tax increase of at least 90 *billion* dollars. (Taxpayers, of course, won't feel this burden until after Election Day 1980.) Tax receipts as a percentage of Gross National Product will be at the highest level since 1944—in other words, at a level necessary to finance a major war. When President Carter talks of "balancing the budget," he clearly means raising taxes to meet increased spending. How he can seriously present such a proposal in the midst of a stagnating economy and an increasingly crushing tax burden, particularly on low and middle-income people, is quite simply beyond me.

Carter's proposals and programs for fighting inflation reveal a similarly shocking willingness to manipulate the American people. Carter has presided over an inflation rate which has grown from 4.8 percent in 1976 to 18 percent in early 1980 and, as discussed in a previous chapter, the federal government alone is responsible for creating inflation through its expansion of the supply of available money and credit. Yet Carter has persistently and publicly blamed every conceivable group in society—business, labor, foreign powers, and even consumers—for inflation, without once acknowledging that federal monetary policy was at the root of the problem. It's appropriate to recall the cynical memo that presidential advisor Stuart Eizenstat wrote to Carter in the midst of the "energy crisis," in which he advised the president, bluntly and straightforwardly, to "scapegoat the Arabs" for domestic problems such as inflation. Carter indeed followed this advice, behaving as though the Arabs controlled the Federal Reserve System or ran the printing presses at the U.S. Treasury.

But it is in the area of foreign policy where Carter's errors have assumed truly disastrous proportions. As has been noted previously, recent foreign policy decisions are fundamentally linked with Carter's energy policy—a policy which has produced precisely the opposite effect from his stated intentions. In his efforts to protect what he has labeled "vital American interests" in the Middle East—which can only mean Middle Eastern oil—he has aggravated a tense situation to the point of confrontation with the Soviet Union in a battle of words, maneuvers, and counter-maneuvers which has been described as "Cold War II." At the same time, the Carter foreign policy has extended its impact to the domestic scene by generating a level of taxation and control reminiscent of wartime and by disrupting the lives of young Americans through the reinstatement of national registration for the military draft.

The most visible event to affect Carter's foreign policy was the taking of 53 American hostages by Iranian militants in the U.S. embassy in Tehran. As I have tried to show, this was the end-result of a troubled history of relations between the United States and Iran. The tragic hostage situation, once it occurred, had no easy solution. The disposition of the hostages was beyond American control; there were no absolute guarantees that any action, diplomatic or military, would result in their freedom rather than their deaths. There was no clearcut solution, but only a choice among options which bore varying degrees of likelihood of success. The only option which was totally unacceptable, in my view, was military action which would have assured the death of the hostages at the hands of the militants, and would probably have led to the taking of other hostages from among the hundreds of Americans still in Iran.

The greater tragedy, however, was the fact that Carter could have prevented the taking of the hostages. His administration had been warned by no less an authority than the former Ambassador to Iran, William Sullivan, himself a former victim of attack by Iranian militants, that to allow the deposed Shah of Iran into the United States would be to physically jeopardize the U.S. embassy and its personnel. Carter's administration was likewise forewarned by the example of Mexico, which withdrew its personnel from its embassy in Tehran and turned its diplomatic affairs over to the Swiss before allowing the shah into Mexico. Yet Carter permitted the shah to enter the United States without having taken the simple precautions which he knew were his to exercise.

Speculation about Carter's motives in the Iranian crisis quickly reaches the bounds of credulity. The political facts are that Carter was behind 2-1 in the polls in his own party before the hostages were taken, and that this margin quickly reversed in his favor at the height of the crisis, as Americans "rallied around their president." Could Carter have simply blundered into a favorable political position by miscalculating the effect of allowing the shah into the country?

Miscalculated or not, Carter's actions before, during, and after the crest of the Middle East crisis show his commitment to a foreign policy of interventionism, confrontation, and conflict rather than a policy of peace, openness, and leadership in reducing tensions. Carter's foreign policy is fundamentally no different from the policy of his predecessors, just as his domestic policies reflect the traditional propensity toward taxing, spending, and regulation which is the hallmark of the politics of the past.

In a campaign year which has seen two guardians of old-style politics, Reagan and Carter, win their parties' nominations, it is not surprising that such a candidate as John B. Anderson has surfaced. Rightly perceiving that a Reagan-Carter choice would alienate millions of American voters, Anderson has leveraged his candidacy for the Republican nomination into a slickly packaged Independent campaign. Like Carter, whose basic campaign theme is that he is less frightening than Reagan, Anderson has pitched his message to voters who would prefer to choose among three evils, rather than the more traditional two.

In the early months of 1980, when he was still a Republican, Anderson made his mark by taking stands on issues which were unpopular with the audience he happened to be addressing. He won high praise for telling a group of gun owners (and national news media) that he favored gun control; this one incident was sufficient to earn him the label, "politically courageous."

Voters should stop to consider this particular example of just how bankrupt the political system has become. For Anderson, in his appearance before the gun owners, was doing nothing more than *telling the truth*; Anderson is in fact on record as favoring gun control and it would have been ridiculous for him to say otherwise. Imagine a typical American voter at a dinner party whose friends ask him his opinion on a political issue; if he goes ahead and delivers his honest opinion, should he then be lionized as "socially courageous"? Of course not—yet John Anderson's reputation for "political courage" has arisen for behavior which is no more remarkable. This situation should not be viewed as a tribute to Anderson, but rather as an indictment of his political colleagues.

Since his days as a Republican candidate, however, it's interesting to note how far Anderson has descended from his pinnacle of political courage. Since declaring an Independent candidacy, Anderson has followed the advice of his experienced advisors and devoted little of his efforts to discussing issues or solutions. He has instead grabbed his share of the Politics of Manipulation by running a negative campaign against Carter and Reagan, joining them in the hope that they won't be held accountable for the specifics of their policies, and content to ride on a carefully built image rather than a carefully considered set of solutions.

In this age of politics, the courage to state an opinion is certainly a virtue, and one which Anderson fleetingly held. But an even greater virtue is *being right*—correctly perceiving the cause of a problem and developing a specific means for solving it.

By this standard, Anderson fails on most major issues. Over and over again, he grants to government the duty, authority, and capacity to solve our problems, and is, in fact, far more ready to do so than Carter or Reagan. He is quite clear about his confidence in government. And, equally clearly, he is wrong.

Consider his proposal to impose a tax of 50 cents per gallon on gasoline—a proposal which helped him win the "Political

Courage" medal back in the days when he was discussing issues. According to Anderson, this tax would decrease gasoline consumption and thus promote conservation. At the same time, the additional revenues from this tax would be earmarked for the Social Security fund, and the taxes paid by individual Americans for Social Security would correspondingly decrease.

In principle, this proposal merely shifts the tax burden around, penalizing people who drive cars and replacing the economic law of supply and demand in energy with a federal directive. That is, it is a frighteningly logical extension of the kind of national energy policy which, as I have pointed out, has driven us to the point of constant crisis.

In practice, the Anderson proposal is guaranteed to fail in its own objectives. For if the tax does in fact succeed in cutting gasoline consumption, then the revenues from gasoline will begin to decrease, thereby cutting the revenues for the Social Security payments, and necessitating new rounds of Social Security tax increases to make up the difference

The Anderson 50-cent-per-gallon proposal is really just a new version of a very old game—the "shell game" played at carnivals. This time, the "pea" is the net tax burden borne by individual Americans, and the "shells" are the different kinds of taxes which government imposes. The people who run shell games are frauds, and so are politicians who try to tell you that tax shifts are equal to real tax relief.

It's noteworthy that Anderson has managed to sidestep virtually every issue that is really fundamental to the long-range solution of American problems. How does he propose to deal with inflation? How does he plan to change the pattern of American foreign policy failure? How does he intend to reduce the burden of government taxing and spending? And how can he present himself to the American voters as a "difference" or a "new alternative" without identifying the basic causes of our problems and challenging them with specific, detailed solutions?

Anderson has no real program to stop inflation. Like Reagan and Carter, he says he wants to slow the rate of increase of federal spending. But he opposes attempts to require a balanced budget, and he says nothing of stopping the expansion of the money supply.

Anderson has no discernibly different foreign policy. Like Reagan and Carter, he accepts the basic premises of interventionism. He appears to be somewhat less militaristic than Reagan—not a difficult stance to adopt—and possibly less erratic than Carter—again, not a tremendous challenge. But he seeks no reductions in the military budget, nor does he redefine our military objective toward a real defense of the United States. And his statements during his summer trip to the Middle East were so palpably politically motivated that thousands of voters who had at first been attracted to his candidacy saw him in a much less favorable light.

As for domestic policy, Anderson sees no real danger in the size of government. He opposes a general tax cut, and believes that government should do more for Americans. In a recent interview Anderson said that he holds a "conception of government as an instrumentality that can function effectively and creatively as a problem-solver. . . . that activist model of what government can be." This is just misleading rhetoric used to disguise the tired old New Deal approach to government. Government is not a problem-solver, it is a problem-*creator*—and after all the failures of government, John Anderson doesn't seem to have learned that lesson.

John Anderson, like Jimmy Carter and Ronald Reagan, has cheerfully exchanged substance for style. Voters are hard pressed to describe his programs to solve major problems—but they know that he favors "sacrifice." They know that Anderson believes that we should have less prosperity, less comfort, and less enjoyment in our private lives, and that somehow this collective deprivation will solve our problems.

Calling for individual Americans to "sacrifice" even more than they have been forced to already to alleviate the very problems which government has caused in the first place—this, too, is part of the Politics of Manipulation, an attempt to shift responsibility for problems to their innocent victims.

Ronald Reagan. Jimmy Carter. John Anderson. Throughout their years in public life, throughout their terms as executors of government power, these men have always been *part of the problem.* To the limited extent that specific issues are discussed, these three candidates sometimes differ, sometimes agree. But their fundamental approach to solving problems is the same: using the power of government. And their fundamental approach to the 1980 presidential campaign is the same: style over substance, image over issues, interest groups and voting blocs over individuals. Each of them hopes to be elected president, not on the basis of his specific solutions to specific problems, but rather on his ability to appear more engaging and less dangerous than the other two candidates.

A crooked card game lasts only so long as the players fail to recognize that they're being victimized. When they refuse to be victims any longer, the cheater is exposed and the game is over.

So must the Politics of Manipulation be exposed and ended. The victims—American voters and taxpayers—must refuse to participate. They must stop giving their reluctant endorsement to any candidate who practices the politics of the past, just as an honest card player would agree to play at a table just because the dealer there is somewhat less crooked than the dealers at other tables.

In my view, the American people deserve a better choice than that offered by Reagan, Carter, and Anderson. They deserve the hope of living their lives at peace with each other and with the rest of the world, the opportunity to better their conditions, and the prospect of taking responsibility for their own decisions and actions. And they surely deserve better than to be called upon to sacrifice and suffer as a result of the errors, miscalculations, and misperceptions of their political leaders.

We have it in our power to end the Politics of Manipulation. If we choose to do that, we can then hope to create a society of peace, prosperity, and freedom. The time has come for a new beginning.

CHAPTER 11:

A New Beginning

If we are to solve America's problems, we must have a new beginning, and head in a Libertarian direction.

In previous chapters, I have shown that the traditional view of government as the ultimate problem-solver is fatally flawed and destined to intensify and expand our problems, not to solve them. I have set forth my specific proposals for dealing with our particularly pressing problems. And I have noted how, in this presidential campaign of 1980, three other significant candidates fail not only to approach problems in the new, creative way that we need, but also fail to rise above the level of traditional politics in America—the Politics of Manipulation.

I'm convinced, of course, that taking a Libertarian approach to each of our important problems will begin rapidly to solve them. And I'm certainly convinced that the American people deserve far better than for traditional politicians to view and treat them as helpless victims of a con game. We can change the course of politics in America.

But even more than this, we can actually change the course of American society—of our quality of life, of the way we interact with other human beings.

When we begin truly to solve the problem of inflation, for example, we will do far more than to stop the overall increase of prices of goods and services. When inflation stops, our whole view of economic life will change.

The average worker can anticipate a pay raise based solely on merit and ability and increased productivity, not the desperate struggle just to stay even with the Consumer Price Index.

The retired person can look forward to years of dignity and independence, not a losing battle between a fixed income and a relentless decline in purchasing power which can only increase dependence upon the very government which created the problem.

The young person about to enter the work force can expect years of virtually limitless opportunities which spring from a healthy, growing productive sector, not a future of uncertainty, confusion, and choices limited by an inflation-strangled economy.

Take another issue: foreign policy. When we take a whole new approach to foreign policy, redefining our military objectives toward defending the United States and ending intervention, we will accomplish far more than saving billions of dollars and avoiding a series of agonizing crises.

For all Americans, and for the first time since the Nuclear Age began, we will actually reduce the risk of armed confrontation, particularly nuclear war, with another superpower. That means that our families, our friends, and our co-workers are less likely to have their lives disrupted, devastated, or destroyed by a tragic event over which they have no control

All of our pressing problems, when we begin truly to solve them by striking at their roots, can change from sources of frustration and despair to sources of new hope, leading not only to improvements in our personal, material circumstances, but also to the restoration of those positive values which are an integral part of the American Dream.

Think of the values we can reestablish in American society by changing our course and taking a new approach which leads to the solution of our problems—dignity, independence, opportunity, freedom, peace.

These values have always been part of American society—but they have been obscured over years of growing control, power, deception, and manipulation by government and those who use government to further their own ends at the expense of others.

As a candidate for President—and also as the parent of a young boy—I want to remove the obstacles which prevent us from bringing such values to the forefront of American society.

Government will not remove these obstacles, and government cannot restore these values.

No legislation ever created dignity or independence. No administrative edict ever brought about equal opportunity. No regulatory agency ever restored freedom. No federal task force ever ensured peace.

But legislation, administrative fiats, regulations, and bureaucratic pronouncements have all done tremendous damage not only to the American Dream and its supporting values, but also, at the most basic level, to the lives of individual Americans.

As George Washington said nearly 200 years ago, "Government is not reason; it is not eloquence; it is force! Like fire, it is a dangerous servant and a fearful master." Politicians who view government as a problem-solver are really viewing the use of government *force*—laws, edicts, regulations—as solutions.

But this view is not confined merely to politicians and bureaucrats, for every individual or interest group which seeks to use government for favor or privilege is in effect invoking the use of government force for its own ends. The victims of this use of force are those who must pay it—either directly through taxation or indirectly through the process which we call inflation.

The use of government force has become institutionalized in American society. The individual who wishes no more than to make his or her own way in the world, without welfare, subsidies, grants, guidelines, or administrative approval has been part of a vanishing species—the free, independent American.

Consider what is still a prevalent attitude among Americans, regardless of their political, economic, or social positions. "Everyone else is getting their piece of the government pie; I might as well get mine, too." This attitude is understandable, for the person who doesn't join the scramble for government bounty will end up a *net loser* to those who do, stuck with an ever-increasing share of the bill while getting little or nothing in return.

This process is illuminated whenever businesses, unions, or other interest groups come to Washington to lobby for special privileges, for themselves or ostensibly for other groups. Actual cash grants are only a small portion of the government treasure chest; far more common are devices such as protective legislation, regulatory exemptions, loan guarantees, tariffs, exclusive rights, and limitations imposed upon competitors.

The really insidious feature of this merry-go-round of competing interests is that each grant, subsidy, tariff, exemption, and protective device, taken by itself, constitutes only a minuscule portion of the average taxpayer's bill. Legislation which subsidizes a particular industry to the tune of ten million dollars, for example, costs less than ten cents per taxpayer. So who cares if that particular legislation gets passed—we'll hardly feel it!

Each such law, regulation, exemption, or privilege implemented on behalf of one interest group encourages other interest groups to follow suit. Why should they sit idly by and pick up the tab while someone else benefits?

The capacity of American taxpayers and our economy as a whole to support this growing morass of regulation and privilege is rapidly reaching its breaking point. The level of inflation and direct taxation is far too high, and it must be reduced and reduced again!

To achieve this, we can't allow ourselves to be diverted by proposals or reforms which don't strike at the root of the problem. Liberal and conservative politicians alike, sensing the strain on our capacity to shoulder the burden of subsidy and special privilege, have suggested means to limit the growth of government. One such proposal is to restrict the rate of growth in taxing and spending to a fixed percentage per year; but that's like suggesting that a speeding locomotive crashing headlong downhill should be permitted to accelerate at a certain rate. Another suggestion is to freeze the level of taxing and spending; but that's like saying that the locomotive should be allowed to continue downhill so long as it doesn't go any faster

No—we should reject these halfway measures and pseudo-solutions. We must stop the growth of government now, and then start to roll it back and diminish its size.

What allows these subsidies and privileges to grow and accelerate? Fundamentally, it is the use of *government force*. The use of force—whether it is to bail out a businessperson or to aid a broad social sub-group—tends to legitimize the further use of force to benefit other broad or narrow interests. Thus we see the process which has developed over many decades in America, and which has brought us to the current state of chronic social, economic, and foreign crisis.

I totally reject the notion that government force is either moral or practical as a means of solving our pressing problems. Force—legislation, edicts, and all the rest—doesn't end poverty, conserve resources, bolster the economy, or reduce international tensions.

Most important of all, force does nothing for—and in fact works against—the establishment of positive values. The use of force is antithetical to the promotion of dignity, independence, opportunity, freedom, or peace.

If the use of government force, then, is arrogant, ineffective, and counterproductive in solving problems and creating a better society, what is our alternative?

Simply put, the alternative—the Libertarian alternative—is *freedom.*

Freedom. The right to choose. The right to make decisions for ourselves. The right to accept responsibility for our own actions. The right to solve personal and social problems voluntarily, directly, and effectively.

My overriding goal is the establishment of this freedom and these rights in American society. Throughout this book, and throughout my campaign for the presidency, I have discussed problems and issues, and ways of dealing with them. In each instance, and at every turn, the solutions I propose emphasize increasing freedom and reducing government interference. I believe that by enhancing and encouraging individual freedom—and in no other way—will we begin to take the practical, real-world steps toward solving such problems as inflation, unemployment, poverty, illiteracy, energy shortages, international conflict, and all the rest.

American society has been moving in the direction of control, regulation, and intervention—crisis and conflict, problems and failures—for many decades. For an equally long period, American politics has been moving in the direction of manipulation and deceit, privilege and power. It is time to change course. It is time for a new beginning.

If there were a button I could push to solve our problems, establish positive values, and restore complete freedom in our society, I would not hesitate to push it. But there is no magic button. Instead we must begin, through the political system, a systematic process of reversing our course, rolling back the glacier of government, and implementing our solutions as rapidly as possible.

A key ingredient in this process, and one that is missing from traditional political discourse and day-to-day affairs of government, is *hope*. The present course of society and politics has stripped away all but the last vestiges of hope for a better, more prosperous, more humane, and more peaceful future. But I'm convinced that the application of Libertarian solutions can create a new hope for Americans.

By balancing the budget at much lower levels, we can bring new hope to American taxpayers whose best efforts to move ahead and create a secure future for their families are presently thwarted by the twin evils of rising prices and rising taxes.

By stopping inflation at its source, we can bring new hope to consumers, especially those on fixed incomes, who now face an economic future of uncertainty, dependence, and despair.

By changing our foreign policy to one of non-intervention, we can bring new hope to all Americans, especially to the young, and greatly reduce the constant threat of tensions and conflict, conscription and war.

By creating an energy policy based on economic reality, we can bring new hope not only to people who must drive cars and heat their homes, but also to those who are concerned about our dependence on foreign energy sources and who seek feasible alternatives.

By bringing freedom of choice into education, we can bring new hope to parents and children who are now locked into stagnating, deteriorating public schools because they lack the means to afford voluntary alternatives.

By establishing a voluntary system of social security, we can bring new hope to all who worry that their futures are now being mortgaged to meet the present needs of a bankrupt system.

By breaking the poverty cycle through economic growth, we can bring new hope to the millions of the poor whose desire for progress and opportunity is now beaten back by economic stagnation.

By restoring full civil liberties to all, we can bring new hope to those who wish only to live their own lives peacefully in their own way, and to those for whom the Bill of Rights should be more than just a piece of paper, but rather an embodiment of living principles.

Finally, by breaking free from the Politics of Manipulation, we can bring new hope to voters who despair of finding real solutions, instead of empty promises, for our very real problems

Libertarians today are fanning the spark of this new hope, by combining a principled vision of what American society *should* be with practical, creative solutions to our problems.

Libertarians represent a healthy cross-section of our society, reflecting the rich diversity and individuality of America which, when not interfered with, can produce a strong, free, spontaneous order. They are very young and very old, and all ages in between; they are conservatively dressed professional men and women, blue-jean-clad students, small business owners, farmers, and factory workers. They are suburban home-owners, central city residents, and inhabitants of small towns; they are in the mainstream of American culture, and they are practitioners of alternative lifestyles.

Despite this wealth of diversity and pluralism, Libertarians all share a fundamental tolerance for the peaceful behavior of others, granting each individual the right to lead his or her own life as he or she chooses, so long as the rights of others are not violated. They understand that granting this right to others helps to insure that their own rights will not be violated.

Libertarians are practical idealists. They hold a vision of a better, more open, more tolerant, and more prosperous society not only for themselves, but also for everyone else. They are genuinely concerned about the problems of the poor, the sick, the aged, and the illiterate, and their concern is intensified by their conviction that the actions taken by government to relieve these problems have been at best ineffective, usually counter-productive, and always oblivious to the rights of individuals.

Libertarians come from a diversity of political backgrounds. They are former conservatives who see that a healthy, growing, free economy cannot coexist with a centralized, expensive, national military machine which only benefits entrenched interest groups and feeds upon foreign intervention. They are former liberals who have grown frustrated with the failures of government social programs and who seek the real solutions to human problems which only freedom can provide. And they are people who have never held an interest in politics before—who in fact were repelled by traditional parties and their candidates—until they learned of the new hope of new solutions through the Libertarian approach.

The thousands of citizens who are supporting my campaign and the campaigns of hundreds of Libertarians candidates in every state are charter members of a *new coalition* in American politics. This new coalition bridges the artificial barriers of traditional politicians and interests. No longer must those who favor economic freedom and much lower taxes square off against those who favor a foreign policy of non-intervention, full civil liberties, and opportunity for the disadvantaged—for these positions are not contradictory, as traditional politicians insist they are, but are instead *complementary* and *interrelated*.

The basic Libertarian positions on all the important issues will bring to Americans once again the hope of real, permanent solutions. These basic positions, taken together, will break the present logjam of failed policies and broken promises, and will free up the American political, economic, and social system so that we may begin to build a society of peace, prosperity, and freedom.

Solving our problems, freeing up the system, establishing a new hope for all segments of society—to accomplish this, we must be willing to try a new approach, to chart a different course. We must have a new beginning.

The future of freedom in America demands nothing less

132

CHAPTER 12

Appendix: The Clark for President Campaign

With projected ballot status in each of the fifty states and the District of Columbia, Ed Clark is heading the most serious third party effort in the United States in over half a century. In 1980 approximately 600 Libertarians are seeking office at the state legislative and congressional levels. The Libertarian Party has emerged as the first broad-based national political party to appear in America since the Republican Party in the mid-nineteenth century.

Founded in 1972, the Libertarian Party has from the beginning attracted supporters from across the entire political spectrum. In the party's first serious presidential campaign in 1976, Roger L. MacBride was on the ballot in 32 states and received 174,000 votes—not a large total, but nonetheless more than any other third party candidate.

It was the "off year" elections of 1978 that clearly established the Libertarian Party as something other than a minor party, and demonstrated its potential to create a three party system in America. That year about 200 Libertarians ran for office and garnered over 1.3 million votes. This total was all the more significant because third parties generally lose ground in non-presidential elections. The Libertarian vote was greater than that of all other national third parties *combined*.

In many races across the country in 1978, Libertarian candidates were the balance of power. One candidate, Dick Randolph of Alaska, became the nation's only elected state legislator from a national party other than the Republican or Democratic. Results from the 1980 elections should represent a major step toward equal status in a three party system for the Libertarians.

Many political observers in the media have concluded that the Libertarians have positioned themselves to make a major impact in 1980 and the decade to follow. San Francisco *Ex-*

aminer political reporter Larry Hatfield wrote that the Libertarians are "the fastest growing political party in America and perhaps the most serious third party in this century." *New West* magazine reported that "suddenly people were talking about the Libertarians . . . observers agreed that this could be only the tip of a very large political iceberg." And Nick Thimmesch, writing in the New York *Times*, said "Where both parties seem becalmed of ideas, the Libertarians send fresh gusts . . . the party is far more creative, diverse in approach, and intellectually stimulating than either the Democrats or Republicans."

What these political commentators and many others have observed is the emergence of a serious national third party simultaneously with an accelerating breakdown in support for the two parties that have dominated the political scene in this century. The socio-political trends in America during the past twenty-five years have greatly weakened the two party system and, hence, increased the opportunity for a viable third party to emerge. There has been a steady rise in the number of independent voters—to the point where today they represent a plurality (or close to one, depending on the poll) of the American electorate.

At the same time, the number of non-voters has dramatically increased. The closely contested 1976 Presidential race managed to attract only 54 percent of the eligible voters. Additionally, the majority of Americans between the ages of 18 and 35 have never registered to vote. This younger element of the voting population has steadily increased in size and is potentially much more important than it was in 1960. The Census Bureau reports that over 40 percent of eligible voters in 1980 will be 34 and younger, compared to only 28 percent in 1960. Should younger voters, who are less committed to the Republicans and Democrats, be motivated to vote in 1980, the possibility of a major political realignment is greatly enhanced. According to Arthur T. Hadley, author of *The Empty Polling Booth*, "Because of the present large pool of non-voters, the future of our country could substantially change in any coming election." Even those who do vote and do identify with one of the two major parties are far less committed than they have been in the past. The *National Journal* reports that voters who ''strongly'' identify with the Republicans and Democrats have declined from 37 percent in 1964 to 23 percent in 1978.

John Anderson's independent candidacy has apparently done little to reverse these trends. Fully 41 percent of those surveyed in a June, 1980 New York *Times*/CBS poll said they were dissatisfied with a choice between Reagan, Carter and Anderson. Thus, by any demographic standard or analysis of the voting public, Ed Clark's Libertarian candidacy faces the most potentially receptive electorate of any third party candidacy in recent history.

The Libertarian Party is organized in every state and maintains a national headquarters at 2300 Wisconsin Avenue, NW, Washington, D.C. 20007. Students interested in Libertarian activism should write to Students for a Libertarian Society, 1620 Montgomery St., San Francisco, CA 94111. The leading explicitly Libertarian magazine is *The Libertarian Review*, a monthly, available for $18 per year from P.O. Box 28877, San Diego, CA 92128.

About the Author

Ed Clark is a Libertarian who combines his principled vision with a thorough understanding of the issues. In 1978 he surprised political experts by winning nearly 400,000 votes as the Libertarian candidate for governor of California. Clark won the Libertarian presidential nomination at the party's national convention in Los Angeles, where more than 2,000 people gathered to participate in the progress of this dynamic new political movement. Ed Clark will be the first new party candidate to achieve total nationwide ballot status in over 60 years, and leads a field of over 500 Libertarian candidates for local, state, and federal offices throughout the United States.

An honors graduate in international relations from Dartmouth College, Clark, 50, holds an Ll.B. degree from Harvard Law School. Ed Clark lives in Los Angeles with his wife Alicia and their six-year-old son Edward Jr.

the rise of law students, as we look back on the age of religious wars and persecution in Europe. On the one hand